MEDIA REVOLUTION

A BATTLE PLAN TO DEFEAT MASS DECEPTION IN AMERICA

BRIAN E. FISHER

CORAL RIDGE MINISTRIES

Dr. D. James Kennedy, Founder

Fort Lauderdale, Florida

Media Revolution: A Battle Plan to Defeat Mass Deception in America
By Brian E. Fisher

Copyright © 2008 Coral Ridge Ministries

Jacket and Interior Design: Roark Creative, www.roarkcreative.com

Published by Coral Ridge Ministries
Printed in the United States of America

Coral Ridge Ministries
Post Office Box 1920
Fort Lauderdale, Florida 33302-1920
1-800-988-7884
www.coralridge.org
letters@coralridge.org

Dedicated to the Memory of

DR. D. JAMES KENNEDY

Pastor, Evangelist, Theologian, Leader,
Mentor, and Revolutionary

His love for Christ and man was the
inspiration for this book.

CONTENTS

ACKNOWLEDGEMENTS

Any work of note is never the product of just one person. Dan Philips: thanks for your encouragement, enthusiasm, patience, diligence, and hard work compiling this book. Kathy Gresham: for lightning fast transcription. Melissa Iossifov: for more pages of research than we were able to get through. John Aman, Karen Gushta, Nancy Britt: for fine tuning and editing, plus a great cover. Tom McCabe, Phil Cooke, Michael O'Fallon: for counsel, wisdom, and networking. Linda Grotke, my executive assistant: for your diligence, servant attitude, and for putting up with me. David Russ, Gary Mustian, Carol Mustian: for ideas, insight, and space. Endorsers and contributors—many thanks.

The staff of Coral Ridge Ministries: it is my privilege to work with you as we enter the Media Revolution. The Board of Directors of CRM: for your vocal and tangible encouragement and your prayers. Anne Kennedy and Jennifer Kennedy Cassidy: you so fully supported your husband/father during his lifetime. Thanks for supporting the ministry he founded.

Richard and Janice Fisher: for encouragement, prayers, and editing. Caleb and Zach: for being the two best sons on the planet. Jessica: for your love, patience, support, and baking. You are my very best friend.

To Jesus Christ: for loving me, saving me, and strengthening me.

INTRODUCTION

TRUTH: The body of real things, events, and facts—a transcendent fundamental or spiritual reality.

LIE: An assertion of something known or believed by the speaker to be untrue with intent to deceive.

MEDIA: A medium of cultivation, conveyance, or expression.[1]

We have been lied to. We have been lied to for more than fifty years by a media presence so large, so powerful, and so pervasive that we haven't fully comprehended the effects of its influence. These lies have tainted our thoughts, prompted our actions, and clouded our worldview so much that, in many cases, we no longer recognize *truth* as *true*. We have been deceived.

Media is influence. You and I are likely to agree on that, but do we realize just how strong that influence is? The news and entertainment media are a constant, almost omnipresent, factor in our daily lives. TV, radio, newspaper, books, music, movies, the Internet, and video games—does a day go by that we don't use at least one of these forms of communication? Someone, somewhere is using each of these mediums to get a message across to us. Entities that want us to change our values, opinions, or thinking are using these channels to purposefully move us in a different direction.

For example, the power of the media to sway the public has recently been demonstrated in the rise of what we at Coral Ridge Ministries call "The New Atheism." Christopher Hitchens penned a best-selling book, *God is Not Great: How Religion Poisons Everything*, in which he writes off the Christian faith as "superstition" and likens religion to "racism." Other books that are similarly hostile to Christianity, such as *The God Delusion* and *Letters to a Christian Nation*, are also being promoted. The latter, according to the publisher, "argues for the eradication of religion, at least religion as we know it."[2]

Hundreds of thousands of people have purchased and read these books. It is probable that the majority of these folks are "good people" who pay their taxes, take their kids to school each day, and are friendly to their neighbors. Yet these "good" people are being *encouraged* to become a part of "the eradication of religion." The "religion" that is under attack is the religion held by the founders of America—the religion which affirms the value of life, and promises the gift of eternal life to those who believe in its God through His Son, Jesus. Ironically, it is this religion that inspired our Bill of Rights, giving us our cherished freedom of speech—the very right which allows the new atheists to express their unbelief with no fear of reprisal. This new atheism is using the media to convey its message with conviction and effectiveness, and many Americans are being deceived.

The media shapes our thinking. It reaches into our hearts and heads in surprisingly far-reaching fashion. It is a documented fact that a steady diet of television viewing will inevitably change the way we think. The Family Research Council (FRC) warns that the most powerful effect of the seemingly unending torrent of violence we witness on television is desensitization. Viewers who witness these constant acts of violence are less horrified by their occurrence in real life. "Some viewers," FRC noted, "may even develop a 'bystander' mentality, in which real violence is considered unreal."[3]

Dr. Leonard Eron of the University of Michigan studied the viewing habits of children for decades. He remarked:

> The only people who dispute the connection between smoking and cancer are people in the tobacco industry. And the only people who dispute the television and violence connection are people in the entertainment industry.... Television violence affects [people] of all ages, of both genders, at all socio-economic levels and all levels of intelligence. The effect is not limited to children who are already disposed to being aggressive and is not restricted to this country.[4]

The harmful effect of media on culture is by no means limited to violence. The Parents Television Council cites a RAND Corporation study of nearly 2,000 adolescents which showed that watching sex on TV influences teens to have sex. Youths aged 12-17 who watched more sexual content were much more likely to follow suit in real life. According to the study, those in the 90th percentile of TV sex viewing were almost twice as likely to engage in fornication as those who see very little—such as those in the 10th percentile.[5] The problem is compounded, however, by the fact that children watch an enormous amount of TV and, therefore, the chances of our children seeing sexually explicit behavior on TV are quite high. A widely quoted study by researchers from the University of Kansas notes that children spend more time watching television than in any other activity, except sleep.[6]

Media is influence—thus media logically leads to action. Any effective influence on a person or culture encourages action. Political candidates use media to persuade us to vote for them. Advertisers use media to prompt us to buy their products and services. Interest groups use media to influence popular opinion in favor of their particular agenda. There can be no doubt: The controllers of mass media are using their influence to gradually and purposefully alter the values and principles of our nation.

For the last fifty-plus years, Americans have been spoon-fed lie after lie through the giant megaphone of what I call the MMD—*media of mass deception*. Purposefully, strategically, and insistently, a group of people standing in the shadows behind a vast number of media conglomerates has slowly and methodically tried to silence the Christian church and has encouraged unbelievers to ever-increasing wickedness. The effect on our culture is unmistakable—and toxic.

Detailed books have already chronicled the moral and cultural collapse which has occurred in America since "The Greatest Generation" won its triumph over the Axis powers. This phenomenon is well documented in standard-bearing works such as *Children at Risk*, by James Dobson and Gary Bauer. Our purpose in revisiting this subject is to prove the intentionality of the media's role in America's decay. That decay is evidenced by the ways our culture now behaves that are diametrically opposed to the values Americans held just a generation ago.

If you are like me, you are growing weary of the

decades-long barrage of lies being hurled at us by the so-called "mainstream media."

- We have been told that abortion is about "a woman's right to choose" and not about an infant's right to life.
- We have been told marriage can be between any two beings, as long as they are in a "committed, caring relationship."
- We are told that Hollywood produces movies and television shows filled with nudity, profanity, and violence, because this is what the American people want to see.
- We are regularly reminded that evolution is "a scientific fact" and that the biblical account of creation is a "religious myth."
- We have been told our Founding Fathers were slave-holding deists who were driven by money and power.

Those of us who recognize that these are "lies and more lies," as pastor, theologian, and founder of Coral Ridge Ministries, Dr. D. James Kennedy, has put it, have been told repeatedly that we represent a tiny minority. We have consistently heard that we are fringe fundamentalists and bigoted extremists; we are old-fashioned and out-of-step. To borrow the now-notorious phrase penned in 1993 by *Washington Post* reporter Michael Weisskopf, those of us who hold to biblical, historic Christianity are "poor, uneducated and easy to command."[7] Repeated over and over, these slogans and catchphrases have almost convinced many of us that the vast majority of Americans no longer hold to a Judeo-Christian worldview.

I'm happy to report, however, that the American people are much more in line with Christian values and worldviews than the media would have us think. And I am also delighted to tell you that the media machine, which has been spreading propaganda across our land for more than fifty years, is slowly but surely losing its ability to influence our nation. We will see just how this implosion of current media structures is taking place in the pages that follow.

There are many books outlining the problems in the media of mass deception. This one is different because it goes one step further: it presents a simple, easy-to-follow plan to show you how *you* can help bring truth, decency, and sanity back to the American media. It will show you how *you* can join the media revolution. In Part One we will define and explain the *media of mass deception* (MMD), reveal its tactics, and outline its destructive influence on the American culture. Part Two outlines the "democratization" of American media and presents a plan to restore morality, decency, and truth to it. We will explore how the MMD empires are slowly, steadily crumbling. Newspaper circulation is falling across the country.[8] The major television networks are hemorrhaging viewers at a dramatic rate.[9] Television, radio, print, and Internet content delivery systems are all in the midst of massive transformation. The result is an unprecedented decentralization of power. That power, once held by a handful of media moguls and conglomerates, is now being disseminated to a much larger, far more influential group of people—"We the people." We are watching the "democratization" of the American media occur right before our eyes.

Any opportunity—no matter how golden—is only a dream if it doesn't have a plan. In Part Two we will also outline a strategy for today's Christians to become a part of the media revolution by giving solid, practical counsel on how ordinary people can play a key role in overthrowing the MMD and replacing it with a consistent, virtuous, godly media influence on our families, communities, nation, and the world.

Can you imagine a world where Christ and the Bible are freely taught and widely revered? Can you imagine a media that espouses the value of human life, gives thanks to our Creator for our existence, and exalts whatever is true and noble and right and pure? Can you imagine what influence that kind of media might have on the American culture?

Opportunity abounds for Christians to use the new technologies that are now available for preaching and teaching the good news of Jesus Christ. We have an historic opportunity to shine the light of biblical truth onto subjects such as the sanctity of human life, the central importance of traditional marriage, America's Christian heritage, and the facts about creation. Like a match lit in a dark room, a little bit of loving, absolute truth can dispel a half-century of lies. The time of secular media domination is over. The Christian media revolution has begun!

PART ONE

THE MEDIA OF
MASS DECEPTION UNVEILED

THE MEDIA OF MASS DECEPTION DEFINED

n 1939, MGM Studios released two of the most successful movies of all time: *Gone With the Wind* and *The Wizard of Oz*. Clark Gable's final line in the former movie became famous, largely because in that bygone day the word "damn" still had the power to offend the American public. I wish our ears were still as sensitive today.

The Wizard of Oz, in addition to all its charm, contains one of my all-time favorite movie lines. Dorothy and her friends have returned with the broomstick of the wicked witch, but the majestic voice of "Oz" commands them to go away and come back tomorrow. As the wizard continues issuing forth flame, smoke, and thunderous sound, Toto pulls the curtain away to reveal a little man frantically operating the controls of all the machinery. Then comes the classic line:

Pay no attention to that man behind the curtain. The great Oz has spoken!

Do you ever feel like the media of mass deception is roaring that same line at you today? *America doesn't want God. America isn't interested in truth and nobility and purity. Americans love violence and promiscuity. Americans want multiculturalism, pluralism, and relativism. Americans don't want to learn about their true history; they just want to have their every need and desire satisfied—now. Americans don't care about peace in their neighborhoods, justice, decency, solid marriages, healthy families, or godliness—they want to become gods themselves.*

Then, right in the middle of all the smoke and sound and fury, somebody pulls back the curtain—just for a moment. And behind the curtain sits a small group of godless media wizards, frantically trying to wield their power, using lights, cameras, and action to dishearten, weaken, and silence the populace. Does mainstream America really value what the media says it does? Do the vast majority of television, radio, Internet sites, music, and books really reflect our core values?

You probably remember the enormous impact of Mel Gibson's movie in 2004, *The Passion of the Christ.* Despite the MMD's best efforts to convince Americans to avoid the movie ("too violent," "anti-Semitic," etc.), *The Passion* is still the highest-grossing ($370 million) R-rated film in box office history. (In true irony, Hollywood rated the movie "R" for violence. But *The Passion* attempted to realistically portray the excruciating suffering our Savior endured in the hours leading up to His death.) The movie critics were shocked and secularists across the country were disturbed by the movie's success. Yet it revealed something deeper. Americans are still fascinated and moved by the story of Christ's death and resurrection. The curtain was ripped aside.

In 2006 the curtain was again pulled aside when the folks of Sherwood Baptist Church in Albany, Georgia, determined that God was calling them to make a movie. Working with a budget of $100,000 (*Titanic* had a budget of $200 million), members of Sherwood Baptist produced *Facing the Giants*, which grossed more than $10 million dollars. Through its story about a high school football team, we learn lessons of forgiveness, grace, and perseverance.

"Pay no attention to that man behind the curtain," the media of mass deception desperately bellows. Yet Americans are paying less and less attention to the MMD. They flocked to see *The Passion* and wept. They eagerly went to see *Facing the Giants* and cheered. There can be no question that many Americans are hungry for messages that exalt God and His Word, messages that celebrate courage and righteousness. This has always been true. But does the MMD reflect these values?

Probably the most significant study of the attitudes of members of the MMD was *The Media Elite*, by Robert and Linda Lichter, and Stanley Rothman. Their research on the news media found that:

- 45% of the media described themselves as either atheist or agnostic, compared to only 9% of the general public.
- 89% of the media reported that they seldom or never attend church, compared

to only 25% of the general public.

- 6% of the members of the media reported that they attended church weekly, compared to 42% of the general public.
- 94% of the media either agreed or strongly agreed with the statement, "Abortion on demand should remain legal," compared to 51% of the public.
- 88% of the media thought that "Television is not critical of traditional and religious values."
- More than half—55%—of the members of the media strongly agreed with the statement, "Adultery is acceptable," compared to 30% of the public.[10]

This study was criticized for using too small a sample (240) but a much larger study conducted in 1985 by the *Los Angeles Times* found very similar results. The *Los Angeles Times* surveyed 3,000 journalists working at 621 newspapers and confirmed the Lichter-Rothman results, finding that "Members of the press are predominantly liberal, considerably more liberal than the general public."[11]

Why the "Media of Mass Deception?"
There are many names for this deceptive media presence in America: the secular media, the media elite, the old media, and the mainstream media. When I use the term *media of mass deception* (MMD), I'm referring to the media structures in television, film, radio, music, and print that hold to a vastly different worldview from mainstream America.

I chose the term "media of mass deception" for several

reasons. First, it conveys the sheer size and volume of a media bent on the destruction of America's core Judeo-Christian values. Playing off of the widely used term WMD (weapons of mass destruction), the term MMD represents the danger and volatility of our current media environment. Second, the term denotes a media culture that intends to distort and to lie. And third, there are many incorrect names used for this humanistic media empire. By using them, we unconsciously accept the assumptions they promote.

We must carefully note the nomenclature we use today so that we speak truth, and so that we do not inadvertently promote a secularizing agenda. For example, using the term "mainstream media" actually promotes the agenda of the MMD to convince Americans that it speaks for mainstream America—which it does not.

We must recognize that while the "old" media structures are slowly dying, they still possess great power to deceive. In May of 2007, the Gallup Organization announced the results of a poll that put public acceptance of homosexuality at an all-time high. In 1982, 34% of Americans felt that homosexuality should be considered "an acceptable alternative lifestyle." By 2007, that approval figure ballooned to 57%. The same poll showed that fully 47% of Americans now believe that "marriages between same-sex couples should be recognized by the law as valid, with the same rights as traditional marriages." In 1982, only 27% of Americans responded affirmatively to the same question.[12] The MMD has had a part in causing this cultural shift in American's attitudes and beliefs.

A Powerful Influence

This is a solid example of the enormous power of the MMD to influence the American people. The Media Research Center and others have demonstrated the extreme lengths to which the media of mass deception will go to portray homosexuals in a positive light and to demonize anyone who speaks against the "mainstreaming" of homosexuality. When Marine General Peter Pace, chairman of the Joint Chiefs of Staff and a decorated combat veteran, stated in 2007 that homosexual behavior was "immoral," he was swiftly, sharply, and universally condemned as a "hateful bigot" by the MMD. No matter that General Pace had also said that adultery was immoral. In contrast, the MMD were quite silent when homosexual activists made hateful comments after the deaths of Jerry Falwell and D. James Kennedy in 2007, men who stood courageously for biblical truth, even when it is unpopular.

Is there an American of voting age who does not recall the murder of Matthew Shepard in 1998? The MMD used the story of the killers of Matthew Shepard to smear all Christians who support traditional marriage by insinuating that we had created a climate of "hate" that actually encourages such crimes. "We knew in the newsroom the day it happened, this is going to be a huge story; this is going to attract international interest," one journalist told ABC News. "I remember one of my fellow reporters saying, 'This kid is going to be the new poster child for gay rights.'"[13]

On the other hand, one year later, when 13-year-old Jesse Dirkhising was abducted, sexually assaulted, and killed by two homosexual men, the MMD took no notice; that is, until alternative media sources focused an outraged nation's attention on the double standard.

Both of these events are tragic and complex. The agenda-driven coverage of a tragedy like Matthew Shepard's murder hurts both the Christian community *and* the homosexual community. Christians are labeled as intolerant, bigoted Neanderthals who "hate" homosexuals. A few Christians respond to such rhetoric by stereotyping homosexuals as a fringe group of vicious predators who are attempting to destroy marriage and take over the nation. Neither depiction accurately describes the majority of the members of either community.

One thing is certain—the slanted reporting of stories like the Shepard murder drives a wedge between the two communities, breeding deep distrust and making reasoned, compassionate discourse extremely difficult. As unconscionable as the actions of the killers are, the MMD is guilty of ignoring some details and twisting others in order to influence the general public according to its own agenda. In 2004, ABC News published a report showing that the murder of Matthew Shepard had nothing to do with his being a homosexual. Instead, he was killed during a robbery.[14] Unfortunately, the damage had already been done. The Shepard case had become a *cause célèbre* for hate crimes laws, and the media of mass deception was not going to change that picture.

The extent of MMD's influence can also be seen in the success it has had in reshaping the public's attitude toward Christianity and Christians. A 2007 survey conducted by the Barna Group among 16-29-year-olds revealed disturbingly high levels of hostility toward Christians and their beliefs. Barna reported that, "Among young non-Christians, nine out of the top twelve perceptions were negative. Common negative perceptions include that present-day Christianity is judgmental (87%), hypocritical (85%), old-fashioned (78%), and too involved in politics (75%)—representing large proportions of young outsiders who attach these negative labels to Christians." Some 91% of the non-Christians surveyed believe that Christianity is "anti-homosexual."[15]

Public relations expert A. Larry Ross correctly observed that "We live in an era where the media and the entertainment industry have *carte blanche* in defining reality. If we read it in the newspaper, hear it on the radio, view it on television or see a preface statement that 'information to follow is accurate,' we absorb it."[16]

I raise these points to demonstrate that the MMD still wields enormous influence over social, political, and spiritual attitudes in this country. For decades it successfully shaped our national discourse and thus many of our individual attitudes and opinions. But as it loses its once-total monopoly over the distribution of information, it loses its ability to affect the culture.

Perhaps one of the most telling evidences of this fact is the attitude of Americans toward the killing of the unborn. For over thirty years the MMD has portrayed abortionists as heroic defenders of women's rights and pro-lifers as fanatics who seek to impose their outdated morality on an entire nation. In spite of this, however, a 2006 Zogby International poll showed public support of abortion to be in "sharp decline." While the poll did count a slim majority of Americans, 52%, as favoring abortion, John Zogby called the results "striking." "The numbers were radically different ten years ago," Zogby said. "Ten years ago, maybe just seven or eight years ago, pro-choice forces were in the ascendancy and posted pro-choice numbers in the area of 65% to 68%."[17] Even more telling, a staggering 72% of teenagers (those who have not been exposed to the 35-year drumbeat of pro-abortion news coverage) told the Gallup organization that "abortion is morally wrong."[18] As we will soon see, the sources of information available to pro-life, pro-family Americans were far more limited just seven or eight years ago than they are today. The MMD is losing its influence.

What About the Term "Mainstream Media?"

In his book, *Stop the Presses!*, Joseph Farah argues that using the term "mainstream media" to describe the media elite is a misnomer. Farah, the founder and editor of the news website *WorldNetDaily*, explains that Americans are leaving traditional sources and flocking toward alternate providers, such as talk radio and the Internet, to get good, truthful information.[19] Farah asserts that what you and I are exposed to every day on television reflects the work of a small group of media insiders. Thus we shouldn't use the term "mainstream media" to describe the media of mass deception.

I believe Farah is right on the money. Mainstream America is not represented in the so-called "mainstream media." A *real* mainstream media would represent what America truly values: marriage between a man and woman, the sanctity of human life, public decency, morality, national pride, and a genuine sense of optimism.

The MMD leaders are *delighted* when you and I refer to them as "mainstream," because that demonstrates that you and I believe that they do indeed represent the attitudes of the majority of the American people. So they adopt the term "mainstream" for themselves, because that further convinces us that the MMD simply *reflects* American culture, rather than seeking to *direct* American culture. However, the same Lichter-Rothman survey, *The Media Elite*, that was quoted above, insightfully concluded that "Television creators...seek to move their audience toward *their own vision* [emphasis added] of 'the good society.'"[20] They are not "mainstream"; they are but a small current in the larger tide of popular sentiment. As further evidence of just how small a proportion of the populace the media elite represent, consider the explosive growth of talk radio. The top two talk show hosts, Rush Limbaugh and Sean Hannity, now draw a combined audience of approximately 26 million listeners. During the same period as their ascendancy among radio listeners, the "Big Three" networks—ABC, CBS, and NBC—have experienced a dramatic plunge in their viewership, from approximately 52 million viewers in 1980 to about 26 million in 2006.[21] Joseph Farah is correct; mainstream America is choosing a different kind of "mainstream media."

Nevertheless, before we can consider further just how mainstream America is choosing a different "mainstream media" to replace the media of mass deception, we must gain a better understanding of the tactics of the MMD. We must understand how, in just one generation, Jesus Christ was evicted from music, radio, and print. We must understand how the MMD has effectively labeled the values that were commonly accepted just fifty years ago as "ignorant," "intolerant," and "fringe" for today's media consumers.

2

THE TACTICS OF THE MEDIA OF MASS DECEPTION

The media of mass deception has influenced American culture in an undeniable way. Its influence has tended toward the ways of death, while claiming to be bringing "life." We are all being subjected to its influence in ways that are sometimes subtle, often overt, and without a doubt, profound.

Former Secretary of Education William Bennett has conducted a broad survey of social science research which showed that between 1960 and 1997, American society saw:

- an 865% increase in the number of couples living together out-of-wedlock
- a 511% increase in the percentage of out-

31

of-wedlock births
- a 280% increase in the rate of violent crime
- a 248% increase in the percentage of single-parent families (the United States has the highest percentage of all industrialized nations)
- a 215% increase in juvenile violent crime
- a 160% increase in the total crime rate
- a 155% increase in the teenage suicide rate
- a 115% increase in the divorce rate
- a 33% decrease in the marriage rate
- a 106% increase in the number of children on welfare
- a 59 point decrease in the average SAT score[22]

I would argue that the media of mass deception, more than any other single agent, is responsible for wreaking havoc on the morals and beliefs of the American people in general—and on the Christian church in particular. There are others who would support that claim. In a speech given to the Heritage Foundation, David Kupelian, managing editor of WorldNetDaily and author of *The Marketing of Evil*, said bluntly:

> No institution in America is more complicit, more responsible for making evil look good and good look evil than the news media, because it is the filter through which we all get our information.
> The press has the power to expose and debunk the marketers of evil at every turn. But it also has the power to carry forward

their message and to give it undeserved credibility. And that, unfortunately, is mostly what the press has done for the last few decades.[23]

Along with the news influence, the MMD uses network television, radio, music, and the Internet to promote its humanistic agenda. It uses eight key tactics to alter our thinking and has effectively done so for the past fifty years. It is imperative that we understand these tactics and the ways they have been used to drag our country into a morass of godlessness, sin, and hopelessness.

The first step in solving any problem is to define it. By identifying these eight tactics, you will become a savvy media consumer and be better equipped to utilize the tools I will be presenting in the last section of this book to overturn the media of mass deception. So, please be patient and follow along with me as we unmask the deception and pull back the curtain further to reveal the machinery behind the curtain—the tactics of the MMD.

TACTIC 1 – The Name Game

The "name game" is the media of mass deception's most resourceful way of assigning new names to topics or ideas that will erode positive emotions in the minds of American people and replace them with negative ones. By using semantic twists and turns, often at the expense of correct grammar and good English, the players of the "name game" seek to take a term with positive connotations and use it to promote a concept previously viewed with distaste. They have done this with surprising success in a number of areas.

One of the best examples of this stratagem is the term

"pro-choice." Recognizing that the phrase "pro-abortion" holds little appeal and, in fact, communicates a cold-blooded willingness to be complicit in the killing of an innocent child, the term "pro-choice" was adopted. Back in the 1960s and 1970s, when the MMD set out to convince Americans that killing babies in the womb was a fundamental right guaranteed by the Constitution, they recognized that the term "pro-abortion" did not produce feelings of warmth and sympathy in the minds of most Americans. "Pro-choice," on the other hand, has a vastly different appeal. The notion of "choice" appeals to Americans' deeply ingrained sense of liberty and fairness. The term deflects attention away from the murder of an unborn child and focuses on the patriotic duty of Americans to support a woman's right to life, liberty, and the pursuit of her happiness. Who wants to stand up in the public square and proclaim that they oppose "a woman's fundamental right to choose"?

In the first sentence of this book I stated, "We have been lied to." The term "pro-choice" is one of this past century's biggest lies. The pro-abortion movement never had anything to do with women's rights. They champion the violent, gruesome, often agonizingly painful dismemberment of unborn children, half of whom are female.

I am dismayed by how many Christians have adopted the phrase "pro-choice" and use it regularly. They are perpetuating a marketing slogan that was created by a small group of pro-abortion activists who were scheming to deceive the American public into viewing the killing of the unborn as an advance for women's rights. Years after the term became commonplace, Dr. Bernard Nathanson, one of the founding members of the powerful pro-abortion lobbyist, NARAL (National Association for the

Repeal of Abortion Laws), candidly admitted: "I remember laughing when we made those slogans up." He was referring to the words that have become so much a part of today's public discourse: *pro-choice, freedom of choice, a woman's right to her own body.* "We were looking for some sexy, catchy slogans to capture public opinion," explained Nathanson, who has since become a Christian and is now pro-life. "They were very cynical slogans then, just as all of these slogans today are very, very cynical."[24]

When Christians use the term "pro-choice," they become unwitting accomplices to the pro-death movement's viral marketing scheme. Every time a Christian says "pro-choice," he or she reinforces a repugnant lie. As Christians, we must be discerning in what we hear and what we say. We must be "shrewd as serpents and innocent as doves," as Christ commanded us in Matthew 10:16, so that we are always speaking the truth in love and not advancing an evil agenda—in this case, the murderous and hugely profitable agenda of the pro-death movement.

"Pro-death movement" is the term that everyone who believes in the sanctity of human life should use. It is *not* about choice; it is about killing babies for cash. Do we reach out in love to an expectant mother who is agonizing over the decision to allow her baby to live or not? Do we gently and politely instruct members of the media and the political class who support the killing of the unborn? Do we grieve with those who are convicted by the realization that by aborting a baby they were directly responsible for the death of their own flesh and blood? Do we share the healing, redeeming love of Christ with all these people? My answer to all these questions is, "Yes, of course!" We must always be the fragrance and the aroma of Christ to this culture (2 Corinthians 2:14-16), holding out the hope that is available through faith alone in Christ alone. And we must *refuse* to play the MMD's "name game." We must not support "the marketing of evil," as David Kupelian so aptly calls it.[25]

Another word that the MMD has attempted to redefine is the word "tolerance." As Josh McDowell explains:

> Tolerance has become the cardinal virtue, the sole absolute of our society, and our children hear it preached every day in school and from government, media and their friends. . . .
>
> The traditional definition of tolerance means simply "to recognize and respect (others' beliefs, practices, etc.) without necessarily agreeing or sympathizing" with them. This attitude—that everyone has a right to his own opinion—is what tolerance means to most of us.
>
> But today's definition is vastly different. This *new* tolerance means to consider every individual's beliefs, values, lifestyle and truth claims as *equally valid*. So not only does everyone have an equal right to his beliefs, but all beliefs are equal. *The new tolerance* goes beyond respecting a person's rights; it demands praise and endorsement of that person's beliefs, values and lifestyle.[26]

McDowell warns that the "new" tolerance will ultimately lead to censorship.

For decades, I have addressed millions of
high school and college students about
Jesus Christ and the historical evidence
for his life and resurrection. As might be
expected, I would often get heckled by
people saying such things as, "Prove it!"
and "I don't believe you." But recently I
have witnessed a startling shift. Now my
attacker invariably says, "How dare you
say that?" "Who do you think you are?"
The issue is no longer the truth of the
message, but the right to proclaim it. In
the new cultural climate, any unpopular
message can be labeled "intolerant" and,
therefore, repressed.[27]

Whenever we hear the MMD referring to "hate
crimes," we should recognize another "name game" in
progress. What politician interested in reelection will
publicly declare his or her opposition to legislation
declared to be "protecting American citizens from acts of
hatred?" Yet, in reality, hate crimes legislation is a
subterfuge to suppress and silence the church and to
elevate the rights of some above that of all Americans.

Another example of a "name game" used by the MMD
is "Christian fundamentalism." A "fundamentalist," by
definition, is someone who believes in certain
fundamental tenets of faith. A Christian fundamentalist,
then, is simply a man or woman who believes in the
fundamentals of the Christian faith. The media of mass
deception, however, has recast that term and uses it to
connote extremism. Efforts, such as that of CNN in its
2007 special, *God's Warriors*, to show parallels among
Islamic, Christian, and Jewish fundamentalists, condition

Americans to link the term "Christian fundamentalist" with dangerous and violent extremism. "Right-wing fundamentalists" has become a favorite epithet of the MMD. The media of mass deception regularly uses the "name game" to distort the truth and reinvent issues. Phrases like "fairness doctrine," "insurgents" (in place of "terrorists"), "no-fault divorce" (there is no such thing), "undocumented workers" (much less threatening than "illegal aliens"), references to pornographers as "defenders of the First Amendment," and scores of other examples bear witness to this cynical, calculated tactic.

TACTIC 2 – The Blitz
The "blitz" refers to the sheer volume of repeated MMD messages. It is a bombardment, a constant barrage of the same idea or action step. It is the stuff advertising is made of. After a while we begin to believe the message simply because we've heard it so many times. I have many times succumbed to the effective "blitz" of ice cream and electronics commercials. But "the blitz" can be employed for much more sinister purposes.

There is really no way to say this gently: we human beings are not as smart as we think we are. We are "input-in, input-out" people. A cynic might say we are "garbage-in, garbage-out" creatures. We are heavily influenced by what we take into our minds. This is why God instructs us to meditate on the Scriptures night and day. In Joshua 1:8 the Lord commands Joshua, "This book of the law shall not depart from your mouth, but you shall meditate on it day and night, so that you may be careful to do according to all that is written in it." In Psalm 1:1-2 we read, "How blessed is the man who does not walk in the counsel of the wicked, nor stand in the path of sinners, nor sit in the seat of scoffers! But his delight is in the law of the Lord, and in His law he meditates day and night." We must constantly feed our minds the Word of God, so that "by the washing of water with the word" (Ephesians 5:26) we might become stronger, more literate, more articulate Christians.

We only need to take a quick inventory of our lives to determine how much time we spend in material that is godly and how much we spend in material that is not. In fact, the Bureau of Labor Statistics has done it for us. The average American with preschool age children living in the home spends, on average, just under two hours each day watching television. (That figure is per person, not per household.) That same individual spends a little less than *six minutes* each day on "religious and spiritual activities." If the kids are over eighteen, the time in front of the television (again, these figures are per person, not per family) reaches two hours and fifty-five minutes *every day*, while time spent on religious and spiritual activity is just seven minutes per day.[28]

One author has grimly noted that Americans spend so much time in front of the "boob tube" that we meet the criteria for "substance abuse" in the official psychiatric manual.[29] These painful statistics reveal that we spend a great deal more time "walking in the counsel of the wicked" than we do feeding ourselves on the truth of God's Word.

Many of us have an uncanny ability to convince ourselves that we are unaffected by the media that we are ingesting. That notion flies in the face of everything that we have learned from social science; it certainly goes against Scripture, which warns us that "Bad company corrupts good morals" (1 Corinthians 15:33). Whoever or whatever we spend the majority of our time with will have a profound influence on how we think *and* how we live.

Good health is a very simple matter. If we eat fast-food burgers and fries three times a day for three weeks, we will get very fat and very sick. If, on the other hand, we eat fruits and vegetables and lean meats, we will likely be healthy. The same principle is true with our minds. If we fill our brains with humanistic junk food, the results are inevitable. American Christians *must* acknowledge that when we spend the vast majority of our time consuming some sort of humanistic media—whether we are reading it on the Internet, watching it on television, or viewing movies, or listening to music—that mental and spiritual intake most certainly affects our mental and spiritual output.

Media, over time, subtly and insidiously changes our mindset and our worldview. If we are not regularly filling our minds with Scripture and filling our hearts with Christian truths, we are not being shaped by the Word and by the Spirit; we are being shaped by an ungodly, unbiblical worldview. We are walking "according to the course of this world, according to the prince of the power of the air . . . the spirit that is now working in the sons of disobedience" (Ephesians 2:2).

Bernard Goldberg worked as a news correspondent at CBS for 28 years. Goldberg drew national attention with his best-selling books, *Bias* and *Arrogance*, in which he blasted his former colleagues for the politically correct slant that infects their news coverage. In an interview with our television show, *The Coral Ridge Hour*, Mr. Goldberg vehemently stated:

> I don't want journalists deciding what's right and what's wrong. I don't want them

championing certain causes, because I guarantee you this: they will not champion the causes that a lot of people, conservative people in America, champion. I want journalists just giving us the news and let us make up our mind. And when it comes to making the world a better place, let's leave that to ministers and priests and social workers, not journalists.

As we have already seen, the men and women who control the media of mass deception are doing precisely what disturbs Mr. Goldberg—they champion cultural causes and they do it by "blitzing." They repeat their secular humanist messages over and over again so that we continue to absorb the information that wears us down. We begin to accept it as reality. "Blitzing" is one of the basic techniques of propaganda.

Consider global warming. Ten years ago, the idea of a catastrophic flood caused by the melting of the polar ice cap would have been laughed off as "Chicken Little stuff." Indeed, many of the panic-stricken voices warning us that the end is near were the very same "prophets" of disaster warning us about "global cooling" in the 1970s.[30] Yet in 2007, Al Gore won the Nobel Peace Prize, in no small measure as a result of his movie *An Inconvenient Truth*, a film which a British court has ruled contains nine significant errors. Those errors, the court said, were made in "the context of alarmism and exaggeration."[31] Even the thoroughly humanist *New York Times* cautioned its readers that "some of Mr. Gore's central points are exaggerated and erroneous."[32]

Nevertheless, the global warming movement continues

to gather momentum. Despite a rising chorus of voices in the scientific community that object to the global warming myth, the claim is perpetuated in the MMD that the "global warming theory" is an accepted fact. The "name game" has been brought to bear on this issue and the phrase "global warming deniers" is beginning to gain traction. The unspoken implication is that anyone who objects to the theory of global warming is in the same category as those who deny that the Holocaust occurred during the Second World War.

We even have a month of the year, May, designated as "Green Month." During this month, television shows promote energy and carbon dioxide emission reductions. Hollywood stars are featured in commercials telling us how to reduce emissions. TV network logos are brightly colored green for the month. When we go out to dinner, restaurants give our kids paper placemats proclaiming the importance of "going green" so that we can stop global warming. The "blitz" is on.

The use of this technique is persistent and pervasive in other key cultural contexts as well. The so-called separation of church and state is regularly cited in the media as the constitutional basis for purging Christianity from public life. Evolution is presented as unquestioned scientific fact and fornication and adultery are routinely depicted as the life of every man. One of television's popular dramas, *Numb3rs*, which features a genius mathematician, regularly promotes evolution as fact, unmarried couples living together, and the view that "science is the pinnacle of reason."

The Culture and Media Institute, a division of the Media Research Center, recently documented the 2007 media blitz directed against the celebration of Easter:

- On Easter Sunday, the History Channel questioned whether the Bible is God's revelation to mankind.
- *Newsweek* and National Public Radio chose Holy Week to host debates between atheists and Christians.
- During Lent, *Newsweek* and the *New York Times Magazine* showcased articles on evolution.
- On March 4, the Discovery Channel broadcast a documentary claiming to have disproved Jesus' resurrection from the dead.[33]

The "blitz" promotes the same message, over and over and over again, using as many different forms of media as possible. It is the consistent and persistent delivery of statements designed to wear down the receiver to the point of agreement with the message. It is a very powerful tactic—it works.

TACTIC 3 – Say What?

"Say what?" takes a half-truth and promotes it as a broadly acknowledged fact. Perhaps the most notable example of this ploy is the so-called wall of separation between church and state. Anyone who has read the Constitution knows that the phrase does not appear there, or in any of our founding documents. Thomas Jefferson certainly wrote the phrase, but that does not make the contemporary application of this idea constitutional. Jefferson was not involved in the drafting of the Constitution. He was in France, serving as our ambassador at the time. I suspect that many Americans genuinely believe that our Founding Fathers wanted to make absolutely sure that the church, religion, and God would remain completely divorced from all things political or governmental.

For the record, the modern interpretation of the phrase is false. The phrase "separation of church and state," which has been used as a highly effective legal bludgeon to drive public expressions of Christianity underground, did appear in a letter from Jefferson to the Danbury Baptist Association. Here is the full text of the actual letter.[34] The section in question appears in bold.

> To messers. Nehemiah Dodge, Ephraim Robbins, & Stephen S. Nelson, a committee of the Danbury Baptist association in the state of Connecticut.
>
> Gentlemen
> The affectionate sentiments of esteem and approbation which you are so good as to express towards me, on behalf of the Danbury Baptist association, give me the highest satisfaction. My duties dictate a faithful and zealous pursuit of the interests of my constituents, & in proportion as they are persuaded of my fidelity to those duties, the discharge of them becomes more and more pleasing.
> Believing with you that religion is a matter which lies solely between Man & his God, that he owes account to none other for his faith or his worship, that the legitimate powers of government reach actions only, & not opinions, **I contemplate**

with sovereign reverence that act of the whole American people which declared that their legislature should "make no law respecting an establishment of religion, or prohibiting the free exercise thereof," thus building a wall of separation between Church & State. Adhering to this expression of the supreme will of the nation in behalf of the rights of conscience, I shall see with sincere satisfaction the progress of those sentiments which tend to restore to man all his natural rights, convinced he has no natural right in opposition to his social duties.

I reciprocate your kind prayers for the protection & blessing of the common father and creator of man, and tender you for yourselves & your religious association, assurances of my high respect & esteem.

Th Jefferson
Jan. 1. 1802.

Jefferson was supporting what appears in the Bill of Rights—that the federal government has no business establishing a national religion. The First Amendment was ratified to protect the fledgling United States from the trap that ensnared England—a government-imposed national denomination that was inconsistent with true Christianity. Many Americans are amazed to learn that several individual states did, in fact, have an established church. The First Amendment says that "Congress shall make no law respecting an establishment of religion." No such restriction was placed on the individual states.

It is also fascinating to note that President Thomas Jefferson regularly attended church services that were held in the chamber of the U.S. House of Representatives—including a service he attended just two days after he penned the letter to the Danbury Baptists.[35] For those readers who are struggling to accept the fact that church services were once held regularly in the House chamber (from 1807-1857), let me add that the Library of Congress records that, "Throughout his administration, Jefferson permitted church services in executive branch buildings. The Gospel was also preached in the Supreme Court chambers."[36] Even a cursory examination of our historical documents reveals the Founding Fathers had no intention of evicting God from government as we have done today. The men who drafted our Constitution considered the Christian faith to be essential to good government.

However, the media of mass deception use the "Say what?" strategy to confuse Americans, not to enlighten them. "Separation of church and state" is ripped from its context to support a viewpoint. The late William Rehnquist, former Chief Justice of the Supreme Court, forcefully objected to this usage, saying, "The 'wall of separation between Church and State' is a metaphor based on bad history, a metaphor which has proved useless as a guide to judging. It should be frankly and explicitly abandoned."[37]

"Say what?" is such a successful tactic that the members of the MMD actually begin to believe their own propaganda. In November of 2006, Larry King interviewed Dr. James Dobson, the founder of Focus on the Family, on a number of subjects. During their discussion, King objected to something Dr. Dobson said by using that time-worn phrase, "separation of Church and state." The transcript of their discussion follows:

> KING: But we have a separation of church and state.
> DOBSON: Beg your pardon?
> KING: We have a separation of church and state.
> DOBSON: Who says?
> KING: You don't believe in separation of church and state?
> DOBSON: Not the way you mean it. The separation of church and state is not in the Constitution. No, it's not. That is not in the Constitution. That was...
> KING: It's in the Bill of Rights.
> DOBSON: It's not in the Bill of Rights. It's not anywhere in a foundational document. The only place where the so-called wall of separation was mentioned was in a letter written by Jefferson to a friend. That's the only place. It has been picked up and made to be something it was never intended to be. What it has become is that the government is protected from the church, instead of the other way around, which is that church was designed to be protected from the government.
> KING: I'm going to check my history.[38]

Larry King is a voice that many older Americans trust to bring them honest interviews. And yet this man, a veteran talk show host who has conducted thousands of interviews, apparently was unaware that the phrase "separation of church and state" does not appear in any of our founding documents. He and his peers have been repeating the lie for so long that they forget that they are perpetuating a dangerous distortion. "Today," David Kupelian observed, "we're made to feel that just whispering something about God, the Bible, the Ten Commandments or, heaven forbid, praying on public property, constitutes an illegal 'establishment of religion.'"[39]

TACTIC 4 – A Major Rewrite

The media of mass deception is adept at revising history to suit contemporary purposes. There are two ways they accomplish this; the first is the rewriting of a nation's history in the books that are given to children in the public schools. A little over fifteen years ago, Catherine Millard wrote *The Rewriting of America's History*. Dr. D. James Kennedy wrote the foreword for the book in which he warned that America's history was rapidly being obscured by "an avalanche of lies, distortions, and misinterpretations."[40] Dr. Millard meticulously documented the results of her seven-year investigation into "the crucial subject of America's Christian heritage, symbols, history and evidence and their rapid elimination from the very records of our United States history...."[41] Her conclusion:

> [T]he rewriting and/or reinterpretation of American historical records ... [is happening] in our national parks, monuments, memorials, landmarks, shrines and churches. In some cases, changes are subtle, and in others, blatant.

> It's done through removal of key historic pieces that do not support the current ungodly bias.... And it's also done through emphasis and de-emphasis of historical periods according to what fits a mode. In fact, the history of our founding period has been eroded and eliminated, almost to the point of oblivion.

God and His undeniable influence on the foundation and development of this country have been all but removed from our educational system. If you don't believe me, just look at your kids' public school textbooks concerning Thanksgiving. If you cannot locate the reason why the Pilgrims began celebrating it in the first place (and why it became a national holiday years later), you have just seen the evidence of the "major rewrite" tactic.

But it is not just the rewriting of history that threatens our culture. With the gradual acceptance of postmodernism in Western thinking, major rewrites are hardly necessary. Postmodern thinking considers man to be constantly growing in intelligence and wisdom and no longer in need of understanding the past to reach his future. Thus, history is viewed as less vital to our education and our cultural development. A postmodern MMD doesn't have to rewrite history—it just ignores it.

If man is constantly evolving, what is the point of remembering our past? If we are smarter and better than the generations before us, we can easily reject their wisdom, contributions, and viewpoints. This idea is based on the dangerous and futile fundamental premise that man can, on his own, progress beyond previous generations and attain unity, peace, and prosperity without any transcendent power or influence.

This is "*Star Trek* thinking." I remember watching the original show from the 1960s and then the *Next Generation* in the 1990s. Both Captains Kirk and Piccard, when encountering some alien being, would often refer to the human race back on earth and how it had finally achieved world unity and peace, becoming a model for other worlds in the galaxy. The implication was that humans had finally evolved into a utopian state on their own, with no divine aid or intervention. If there is one thing history *has* proven, it is that mankind is very adept at repeating mistakes of the past and that every generation struggles with our basic human condition—original sin. That sin, friend, cannot be rewritten or ignored; it can, however, be forgiven.

Besides being incredibly bold, the "major rewrite" tactic bears great potential for evil. "Pride goes before destruction," Proverbs 16:18 warns us, "and a haughty spirit before stumbling." To assume that we are somehow "better" or "smarter" than those who went before us is to stumble into arrogance that will lead us toward a catastrophic fall. Every great nation of the past has already proven that. If we fail to learn from the mistakes and sins of the past, we are doomed to repeat them. But if we treasure our history, we will with humility read biblical and historical accounts of the fall of nations and glean from them the lesson that "Righteousness exalts a nation, but sin is a disgrace to any people" (Proverbs 14:34).

Scripture is replete with God's commands to His people to "*remember.*" Throughout the Old Testament we see God instructing His people to build altars or places of remembrance to remind them of God's faithfulness. As Jeremiah recorded, "Thus says the Lord, 'Stand by the ways and see and ask for the ancient paths, where the good way is, and walk in it; and you will find rest for your souls…'" (Jeremiah 6:16). The celebration of the Passover was instituted to remind the people of Israel how God delivered them out of bondage in Egypt, just as the Lord's Supper causes Christians to remember Christ's body, which He gave to redeem us from our bondage to sin and death. Remembering our history is a means that God has graciously provided to lead us down the path of peace and righteousness and to remind us not to become prideful.

Just before he defeated Goliath on the battlefield, David called out, "The Lord does not deliver by sword or by spear; for the battle is the Lord's and He will give you into our hands" (1 Samuel 17:47). It is God and God alone who is "ruler over all the kingdoms of the nations" (2 Chronicles 20:6). If we accept the postmodern notion that history is no longer relevant to our lives today, we are imbibing the humanist dogma that man has evolved beyond the need for the grace of God. When, however, we refuse to walk in the ways of God, rather than "evolving," we descend into a state of total arrogance which, according to Scripture, precedes complete destruction.

TACTIC 5 – "That's Un-American!"

"That's un-American!" is another favorite tactic of the media of mass deception. America is the home of the free, the MMD reminds us. When someone objects to an imagined "right," like the right to publish pornography, the MMD is quick to object, citing free speech and freedom of the press.

It's un-American, we are told, to restrict anything that anyone wants to do. The phrase "freedom of speech" is repeated so often that I wonder if we realize what that freedom guarantees. According to the MMD, our

Constitution guarantees a right to "freedom of expression," so Americans should be allowed to print, paint, or broadcast whatever comes into their minds, no matter how vulgar, profane, or blasphemous. This argument is used to defend publishing the vilest kind of pornography (including child pornography), and to protect the rantings of shock jocks on national radio.

The text of the First Amendment reads:

> Congress shall make no law respecting an establishment of religion, or prohibiting the free exercise thereof; or abridging the freedom of speech, or of the press; or the right of the people peaceably to assemble, and to petition the government for a redress of grievances.

We have become so ignorant of our own history that we no longer remember that the freedom of speech enshrined in the First Amendment was intended to give Americans the right to criticize our government.

Our Constitution created a framework of government in which citizens could petition the government without fear of reprisal. Freedom of the press, as Joseph Farah has documented, was designed to make the news media a watchdog *over* the government, not a public relations office *for* the government. This is why the press used to be called "The Fourth Estate," complimenting the Executive, Legislative, and Judicial branches of government. The media were to be an independent overseer of the activities of government.

This freedom of speech, for which our Founders bled and died, did not mean the removal of all decency and civility. We can be certain that they never dreamed that pornographic pictures of naked children would be made available in public libraries under the protective umbrella of "free speech." *Human Events* recently observed:

> For the last half-century, the Supreme Court has consistently broadened protections for pornographers and child molesters. In 2002, the Supreme Court construed the First Amendment to protect virtual child pornography (*Ashcroft v. The Free Speech Coalition*, 2002)—child pornography produced utilizing computer-generated minors. Striking down the Child Pornography Prevention Act of 1996, the Supreme Court gushed about the possible artistic, literary and social value of child pornography. "[T]eenage sexual activity and the sexual abuse of children...have inspired countless literary works," blathered Justice Anthony Kennedy, author of the majority opinion, citing *Romeo and Juliet*, *Traffic* and *American Beauty*.[42]

For Justice Kennedy to imply that *Traffic*, a movie about a crack-addicted teenage prostitute, is a "literary work" comparable to Shakespeare's *Romeo and Juliet* is of grave concern. Yet this is the opinion of a man who decides cases of law in the United States Supreme Court. Apparently it is Justice Kennedy's opinion that sexually suggestive computer-generated images of children have merit and those who stand against such "expression" are standing against the American way. That is what I call "un-American!"

TACTIC 6 – Odd Man Out

The media of mass deception uses the "odd man out" tactic to make the viewer/listener feel that his or her traditional biblical values are isolated and idiosyncratic. The MMD has blitzed Americans with so many half-truths and outright distortions, and done it with such tenacity, that we start to believe that we are all alone in our objections to anti-biblical values. But our beliefs are always the basis for our behavior. If we perceive ourselves as a tiny minority of traditionalists who hold to outdated virtues and morals, we begin to behave according to that perception. Which of us wanted to be picked last for a schoolyard game of dodgeball? Who wants to be ostracized at a social function? We simply don't like being the "odd man out." So if we perceive ourselves as the *minority view*, we tend to become silent, or we "go along to get along."

Nevertheless, Rush Limbaugh's rise to national prominence has powerfully refuted the "odd man out" tactic. (Quickly now—how many other media personalities can be readily identified by their first name alone?) It is clear that Limbaugh's tremendous rise in popularity was largely driven by the fact that tens of millions of Americans under the influence of the MMD's use of "odd man out" suddenly realized that no such thing was true.

Bernard Goldberg, himself a member of the so-called media elite for 28 years, spoke to one of our *Coral Ridge Hour* producers about the disconnect between the MMD with the American people:

> They're out of touch on so many values

with the American people. You see, the reason I think the media elites are corrupt isn't because they lie and make up stories. It's because they have a set of values ... they're a different set of values than that of Middle America. That's why it's corrupt. They have one set of values. Middle America, by and large, has another set of values, and the media elites, I don't think, respect that other set of values as much as they should.[43]

Brent Bozell, founder and president of the Media Research Center, has made a career of documenting the adversarial tactics of the media of mass deception. His analysis of the mindset that drives "odd man out" is telling:

A career spent studying the news business has shown me that members of the media do have, if not pure hatred, a real distaste for conservatives—not just the political positions they hold, but the people themselves.... At the networks, the major newspapers, and the national magazines, journalists all too often look across the country and instead of seeing hardworking, taxpaying conservatives from all walks of life—polls have told us for years that a strong plurality of Americans call themselves conservatives—they see the unsophisticated, the provincial, people whose dark passions can be easily stirred. They are the "poor, uneducated and easy to command," as former *Washington Post* reporter Michael Weisskopf, now a senior correspondent at *Time* magazine, famously called them....[44]

TACTIC 7 – Silence of the Lambs

The media of mass deception bullies people who hold traditional values into what I call "the silence of the lambs"—thus we keep quiet because we don't want to be seen as intolerant or hateful people. A recent movie, *I Now Pronounce You Chuck and Larry*, provides us with an example of this tactic. The plot is about two heterosexual men who get "married" because one of them needs domestic partner benefits. The movie portrays Christians as bigoted fools who are anti-homosexual, anti-professional, and downright rude. The film also features a pastor who is a bully in the Christian community. What well-meaning Christian wants to be viewed as such?

The Parents Television Council conducted a comprehensive study of 2,271.5 hours of primetime programming on broadcast television during 2005-2006. The results were not surprising:

- Depictions of elements of organized religion such as clergy, doctrine, or laity were mostly negative. Negative characterizations tended to come from scripted dramatic or comedy shows.
- Fox was by far the most anti-religious network. One in every two (49.3%) portrayals of religion on the Fox Network was negative. Long-time champion NBC came in second in negative depictions of religion, with well over a third (39.3%) of

such portrayals being negative. Among other networks, on UPN over a third (35.4%) of depictions of religion were also negative. ABC registered 30.4% and CBS 29% negative portrayals. The WB network featured the fewest negative depictions of religion (21%).

• The number of negative portrayals increased steadily with each hour of prime-time. Negative treatments constituted 31.9% of all treatments in the 8 p.m. hour, 33.9% in the 9 p.m. hour and 44.4% in the 10 o'clock hour.

• At no time during prime time, and on no network did the positive portrayal of religion even hit the 50% mark.

• Devout laity—non-clerical individuals who profess religious faith—were treated most negatively by entertainment programs. Over half (50.8%) of all entertainment television's depictions of laity were negative. Only 26% were positive.

• Close behind in negative portrayal were religious institutions—such as particular denominations, specific religious beliefs, or direct references to Scripture—nearly half (47.6%) of which were negative. By contrast, only 18% of depictions of religious institutions were positive.[45]

The CBS forensics drama *Cold Case* recently centered on a fictitious high-school abstinence club led by a perverted youth pastor and full of hypocritical, sexually-active Christians. The "Christian" youth group ultimately stones one member to death, quoting the Bible as justification for committing murder. "When's the last time your local Christian youth group stoned somebody to death?" Colleen Raezler of the Culture and Media Institute asked.[46]

These negative portrayals have taken their toll on the American consciousness, particularly among unchurched Americans. A 2002 Barna survey found that "[A]mong a representative sample of people who do not consider themselves to be Christian, the image of 'evangelicals' rated tenth out of eleven groups evaluated, beating out only prostitutes." Lesbians (23%), lawyers (24%), and movie and television performers (25%) all received higher favorable ratings than did evangelicals (22%). The Barna Group was quick, however, to point out an anomaly in the survey results. "Born again Christians" (32%) and ministers (44%) received some of the *highest* approval ratings of the twelve groups ranked, rating only behind military officers (56%).[47]

After considering the data, the Barna Group concluded:

> The survey data suggest that people form impressions of others on the basis of one-dimensional images created and communicated by the mass media. "Our studies show that many of the people who have negative impressions of evangelicals do not know what or who an evangelical is," commented George Barna…. "People's impressions of others are often driven by incomplete, inaccurate or out-of-context information conveyed under the guise of objectivity when, in fact, there is a

point-of-view being advanced by the information source."

The research also reveals the power of language. "Somehow, 'born again Christians' have a more favorable image than do 'evangelicals,' although few adults are able to identify any substantive differences between those two groups," noted Barna. "This is most likely a result of the thrashing that evangelicals receive in the media. It seems that millions of non-Christians have negative impressions of evangelicals, even though they cannot define what an evangelical is, accurately identify the perspectives of the group, or identify even a handful of people they know personally who are evangelicals. There appears to be a lot of religious divisiveness in America based on caricatures and myths rather than on the basis of true ideological or theological differences."[48]

Indeed, there are scores of "one-dimensional images" of Christians broadcast by the MMD that are "based on caricatures and myths." Stop and think about it: when was the last time you saw a movie or television program that portrayed a Bible-believing Christian in a positive light? On the other hand, how many movies have you seen where "fundamentalist Christians" are portrayed as delusional, violent, right-wing extremists who use the Bible to justify evil? The MMD works to marginalize the church on the one hand, while simultaneously intimidating the vast majority of Christians into silence on public policy matters. After all, we don't want to be lumped in with the ignorant, violent, bigoted "Christians" we see on the screen.

The "silence of the lambs" is a tactic that has been employed to create the inaccurate stereotype that all Christians are obnoxious, violent prudes who are a danger to a free society. In fact, true Christians are the most loving, compassionate, truthful people on the planet. We certainly aren't perfect, but we serve a Savior who is.

That hypocrisy, violence, and immaturity exist among Christians is regrettably undeniable. That those characteristics represent the entire Christian church is a gross exaggeration and an inaccurate conclusion. The history of the Christian church, though not without mistakes, is full of countless acts of grace, charity, assistance, love, commitment, fidelity, faith, and hope. If the MMD were to ever report the truth of that statement, we would see a monumental shift in public attitudes towards "evangelicals."

TACTIC 8 – Didn't Moses Build the Ark?

The producers of the 2007 animated movie *The Ten Commandments* commissioned a study to see how well the average American could recall God's Ten Commandments, compared with certain bits of cultural trivia. Here are some of the results of the survey, conducted by Kelton Research:

- 35% of Americans can recall all the names of all six Brady kids from TV sitcom *The Brady Bunch*.
- 25% could name all seven ingredients of the McDonald's Big Mac.
- Only 14% could accurately recall all Ten

Commandments.

• Eighty percent of Americans knew that "two all-beef patties" are one of the ingredients of the Big Mac, but fewer than six in ten could recall "You shall not murder."

• Sixty-two percent know that pickles are an ingredient of the Big Mac hamburger, yet only 45% could recall the commandment to "Honor your father and your mother."

• Bobby and Peter, the least-recalled names from the Brady Bunch (43%), were much more memorable to Americans than the least-recalled commandments: "Remember the Sabbath day, to keep it holy" (34%) and "You shall not make for yourself an idol" (29%).

• Even those who attend a house of worship at least once a week struggled to name all Ten Commandments. "You shall not murder" (70%) and "You shall not steal" (69%) were more difficult to recall for this group than the top two Big Mac ingredients—two all beef patties (79%) and lettuce (76%).[49]

"Didn't Moses build the ark?" is a diversionary tactic that keeps us distracted from the basics of our faith. More than twenty years ago, the late Dr. Neil Postman wrote *Amusing Ourselves to Death*. Postman argued that we have become such an entertainment-oriented culture that we have forgotten how to think. The fact that more Americans can remember the names of the fictional characters of a 30-year-old sitcom than can recall God's living and active Word is stark proof of this fact.

We spend seven minutes a day in the Bible, but we sit down in front of a television set for up to three hours a day, watching content that is, by and large, deceptive. A biblically illiterate church is a numb, dumb, silent church. A church that immerses itself in the Word of God is a vibrant, passionate, effective church. How much of the church in America would you describe as "vibrant," "passionate," and "effective"? Sure, most of us can point to a few individual congregations—and if we're blessed, we belong to one of them. But overall, is the church impacting the culture? Or has the culture been far more effective at absorbing and silencing the church?

I do not lay the blame for this ignorance and indifference solely at the feet of the media. If we take a good hard look at ourselves, we must concede that the blame for being distracted and ignorant is our own. Many of our churches have jettisoned their primary responsibility to preach and teach the Word of God. We hold delightful social functions and go to great lengths to make seekers feel comfortable in our assemblies, but when it comes to proclaiming eternal truths that might actually offend us and cause us to repent of our current lifestyles, we shy away. The result is an American church that can readily recall the ingredients of a hamburger, but struggles to explain how God instructed us to live happy, holy lives. We no longer invest our time in the things that are eternal; we spend our time on the things that are material. Dr. Postman was acutely perceptive; we are, indeed, "amusing ourselves to death" by our diversions.

We must remember this important point: the proclamation of true godly principles often hurts and offends. For every person who is humbled and changed by the truth, there are ten who reject it, scorn it, and hate it. That, my friend, is life. In an age where many Christians believe they should make everyone around them feel comfortable, I would challenge them to name one influential figure from the Bible who acted according to that principle. No such model exists. The sharing of God's truth is an act of love and obedience on our part. We should allow nothing to divert us from that task.

3

THE MEDIA OF MASS DECEPTION AND THE CHURCH

Let us now tighten the focus and explore how the tactics of the MMD have directly impacted Christianity in America. During the past fifty years the media has been successful in isolating the church from the culture and convincing Christians that they must remain in their own closeted society.

You may not be aware of the fact that until the mid-1960s the church had a profound role in the content of motion pictures. Ted Baehr and others have documented that for the better part of three decades, from 1933 to about 1966, the script for every movie to be released in the United States was evaluated according to a strict production code. The Hays Code required filmmakers to scrupulously avoid plots and depictions that would glamorize violence and evil. There were three overarching principles governing the code. The first of these read:

> No picture shall be produced which will lower the moral standards of those who see it. Hence the sympathy of the audience shall never be thrown to the side of crime, wrong-doing, evil or sin.

Younger readers may shake their heads in disbelief when they read those words, yet it is historical fact. This production code specifically warned filmmakers to avoid glorifying crime and violence, the use of alcohol and profanity, and more. There was a section of the code which warned filmmakers to treat all religions and religious people with respect. There were a number of specific restrictions on the depiction of sexual activity:

> **SEX**
> The sanctity of the institution of marriage and the home shall be upheld. Pictures shall not infer that low forms of sex relationship are the accepted or common thing.
>
> 1. Adultery, sometimes necessary plot material, must not be explicitly treated, or justified, or presented attractively.
> 2. Scenes of Passion
>   a. They should not be introduced when not essential to the plot.
>   b. Excessive and lustful kissing,

lustful embraces, suggestive postures and gestures, are not to be shown.

c. In general, passion should so be treated that these scenes do not stimulate the lower and baser element.[50]

These were the days when classics like *The Wizard of Oz, Gone with the Wind, It's a Wonderful Life, The Ten Commandments, Ben Hur,* and *The Sound of Music* were made. Charles Schulz's *A Charlie Brown Christmas,* in which little Linus recited the narrative of the birth of the Christ child from the Gospel of Luke, was made in 1965. For thirty years filmmakers voluntarily submitted themselves to the Hays Code, because they feared that the government might step in and impose even stricter guidelines if a public outcry arose over immorality portrayed in films.

Then in 1966 the Hays Code was abandoned. Accounts of why this occurred paint an intriguing picture. Jack Valenti took over as president of the Motion Picture Association of America (MPAA) in 1966. "The first thing I did," Valenti boasted, "was to junk the Hays Production Code, which was an anachronistic piece of censorship that we never should have put into place."[51] In 1968, Jack Valenti and the MPAA unveiled the ratings system that, with only a few changes, remains in effect today.

Joseph Farah identifies a different culprit for the change. Farah says that the church essentially abandoned the movie business, *over the objections* of the industry leaders. In his book *Taking America Back,* Farah states that the National Council of Churches claimed that it could not afford the $35,000 a year that it cost to maintain the

Protestant Film Office, so the panel of religious leaders who had once held the movie industry in moral check walked off the job.[52]

Freed from the restraints of the Hays Code (which *The New York Times* called "draconian and increasingly outmoded"[53]), the moral quality of movies deteriorated almost overnight. In 1965, the Academy Award for Best Picture went to *The Sound of Music*. Just four years later, the Academy deemed *Midnight Cowboy*, an X-rated movie about a homosexual prostitute and his pimp, to be the best picture produced in the United States during 1969.

Respected *Movieguide* reviewer, Tom Flannery, chronicles the sweeping degeneration of Hollywood that occurred in the late 1960s:

> With the success of early new wave hits like *Bonnie and Clyde* and *Easy Rider*, gratuitous sex and violence became rampant in major mainstream pictures, along with, in many cases, the virtual nonstop use of profanity and blasphemy. All in the name of "keeping it real."
>
> Recreational drug use became commonplace and religious faith came under fierce attack—at first in declarations of atheism by hip and attractive young couples (*Love Story*) or angry denunciations of God by heroic lead figures (*The Poseidon Adventure*), but eventually to the most vile, obscene and unspeakably blasphemous assaults against Christianity, and Christ Himself, imaginable (*Dogma, Saved!* and of course *The Last Temptation*

of Christ, among many others).

What was once considered shockingly inappropriate was now par for the course.... The new wave movement had essentially transformed the film industry into a vehicle for political activism and social change.[54]

Hollywood asserts that the degrading and immoral material it is currently foisting on America merely reflects our own tastes and desires. Film critic Michael Medved has been telling audiences for years that this is a lie. Medved insists that one need look no further than box office receipts to test the truth of his claim. In his book, *Hollywood vs. America,* Medved writes:

> In 1967, the first year in which Hollywood found itself finally free to appeal to the public without the "paralyzing" restrictions of the old Production Code, American pictures drew an average weekly audience of only 17.8 million—compared to the weekly average of 38 million who had gone to the theaters just one year before! In a single twelve-month period, more than half the movie audience disappeared—*by far* the largest one-year decline in the history of the motion picture business.[55]

Despite disastrous economic outcomes, Hollywood has continued to pump sewage into a culture that continues to reject what Hollywood is selling. Ted Baehr and Pat Boone recently shone the bright light of truth on an industry that is nosing over into a death-spiral. In their book, *The Culture-Wise Family*, Baehr and Boone reference that the five pictures nominated by the Academy for Best Picture in 2005 combined for the lowest box office grosses in *twenty years*. And it wasn't just these five stinkers that failed to entice moviegoers. Overall box office receipts dropped a whopping six percent that year.[56]

Jody Eldred is a thirty-year veteran of the television industry and received an Emmy Award in 2004 for his work for ABC News. He asks:

> Did you know that nine out of ten Hollywood films lose money? Did you know that the vast majority of new television shows are cancelled because no one is watching them? Do you wonder why...? Because the people creating them are completely out of touch with the people they are creating them for! Their worldview is vastly different from the worldview of most Americans. We have a largely Christian nation, but Hollywood is largely un-Christian, and in many, if not most cases, anti-Christian. They're not just out of touch. They're against you.[57]

Retreat from the Culture

The very same pattern of moral disintegration seen in Hollywood can also be clearly traced in the music industry. In the 1950s and 1960s Pat Boone, Elvis Presley, Johnny Cash, and others sang gospel songs. Just as Christian-themed movies like *Ben Hur* would dominate the Oscar awards, gospel music competed aggressively for the top Grammy Awards. Then the Beatles burst onto the American scene. A friend of mine who grew up in that generation once told me:

> The Beatles crooned to us in 1964, "I Wanna Hold Your Hand." It all seemed so fresh and fun and innocent. Just *four years later* we were still singing along to "Why Don't We Do It in the Road?" And I'll bet you that not one of us even stopped to think about just what kind of a Pied Piper's journey they had led us on.

Where were the Christians during this disastrous moral freefall of our popular culture? Why did the church suddenly abandon its mandate to shine the light of biblical truth on the unfruitful deeds of darkness (Ephesians 5:11-13)? Perhaps one reason was a misreading of the admonition of 2 Corinthians 6:17: "Therefore, 'Come out from their midst and be separate,' says the Lord. 'and do not touch what is unclean; and I will welcome you.'" Many godly people recoiled from a culture that they rightly recognized as increasingly unhealthy for them and their children. Instead of attempting to infiltrate the media and recapture the territory that had been surrendered in the 1960s, many in the church began to believe that they should thrust the media away and withdraw from the world.

While understandable, even laudable, this desire to "keep oneself unstained by the world" (James 1:27) represented an unbiblical retreat from the culture. If Christians are to obey the Great Commission (Matthew 28:18-20) and the Cultural Mandate (Genesis 1:26-28), we must *engage* with the culture, not retreat from it.

The media of mass deception took advantage of the church's flight. As Christians continued their exodus out of various media realms during the 1970s, Marxism and secular humanism came flooding in to fill the void. The church maintained its silence on major cultural events— music festivals, the sexual revolution, and the ever-increasing radicalization of American political thought.

In 1967, for example, there was great concern over a Beatles' song titled, "Lucy in the Sky with Diamonds." The British Broadcasting Corporation actually banned the song, because the title's initials (LSD) coincided with the name of the dangerous hallucinogenic drug that was stealing the minds of young people. Shortly thereafter, by the close of the 1970s, songs with titles like "Runnin' with the Devil," "Highway to Hell," and "Cocaine" filled the airwaves. The church whispered disapprovingly from within the walls of its sanctuary, but was still stubbornly withdrawn from the godless subculture that was threatening to envelop the West.

The Birth of the "Christian Ghetto"

Confronted with the choice of "fight or flight" in regard to the cultural chaos, the Christian community, by and large, chose flight. We didn't stop watching television or listening to music, however. Instead, people who held to a Christian worldview began to develop their own parallel media universe. In the music industry, for example, an entirely new genre of Christian music sprang up in the late 1970s and early 1980s. Artists like Keith Green, The 2nd Chapter of Acts, Mylon Le Fevre, and Petra attempted to call America's youth back to their godly roots and biblical heritage. These artists saw the need for Christian music to once again infiltrate the culture and thus a new segment of the music market was identified—"Christian music."

Just a few decades earlier there was no such thing as "Christian music." The Christian worldview was evident in the big band sound, R&B, jazz, and gospel. But in the '70s and '80s, Christian music sprang up as an "alternative" to secular music. Instead of permeating the musical culture, Christian music became a separate genre unto itself. Christian music companies produced Christian music to be distributed in Christian stores and played on Christian radio.

I worked in Christian radio in the mid-1990s and I watched a sizeable and positive change take place in the Christian music industry. For years Christian music companies had been roundly criticized for poor quality, little creativity, and bad marketing, and they suffered financially. Then a fantastic change began to occur. Christian artists started to get airplay on secular radio— again. Michael W. Smith, Amy Grant, BeBe and CeCe Winans, dc Talk and a few other groups came out with hit songs that drew attention from the secular radio stations.

To my dismay, however, many of these artists were panned by the church and Christian publications. When they were played on secular stations, they were labeled "crossover artists," as if they had somehow betrayed Christianity by jumping ship and "crossing over" into secular realms. When Michael W. Smith's "Place in This World" shot up to number five on the pop charts in 1990, he was widely criticized for moving into secular radio.

I am reminded of the criticisms directed at Jesus for associating with tax collectors and sinners rather than staying within the confines of the synagogue. Jesus reproved His critics, "It is not those who are healthy who need a physician, but those who are sick" (Matthew 9:12). Musicians like Smith had to be shaking their heads in disbelief. Although using their talents to be obedient to Christ's command to "Go therefore and make disciples of all the nations" (Matthew 28:19), they were being blasted, not by the media of mass deception, but by the very people who should have been celebrating and supporting their outreach.

These artists were the pioneers of their time, paving the way for other bands like Jars of Clay, MXPX, Switchfoot, and Casting Crowns to enjoy exposure to a widely secular audience, thus fulfilling our obligation to bring Christ into the culture by all means possible. The process certainly hasn't been perfect; but at least a partial proclamation of the Christian worldview has once again been finding its way back into the music industry. Still, there is tremendous cultural pressure exerted on Christian artists to remain separate from the larger culture. We have Christian music and non-Christian music; Christian television networks and secular networks; "regular" search engines and Christian search engines; Christian bookstores and non-Christian bookstores; Christian video games and secular video games.

Although the influence of Christianity declined throughout the twentieth century, it was the 1960s that accelerated the process. Prior to that pivotal decade, the Christian worldview was more broadly accepted, even encouraged, in the media. It provided perpetual "salt" for our culture. Today the opposite exists. The Christian worldview has been segregated into its own subculture and is being forced to find ways to reform a much larger and more powerful secular media presence.

Silencing the Church

Emboldened by the church's voluntary retreat from the marketplace of ideas, an increasingly anti-Christian media has become more aggressive in its push to evict the church from the culture. Since it was already in retreat, the MMD has taken the opportunity to proclaim that the church doesn't belong in the worldly affairs of the culture, and too many pastors and congregants have accepted that lie.

I recently had lunch with two ladies who are heavily involved in a national network of crisis pregnancy centers. We were discussing Coral Ridge Ministries' *Ten Truths about Abortion* project, which equips and encourages the church to engage in the battle for the lives of unborn children. During our conversation, one of the women said to me:

> Do you have any idea how many pastors won't say *anything* from the pulpit about abortion? We know people who attend these churches; they've been out to the clinics, trying any way they can to turn these young ladies away from killing their babies. And they'll go to their pastors and ask them to say *something* to get the flock to thinking about this issue and praying about it, and the answer is "No." They don't want to talk about it. They don't think it's "appropriate." The irony is that some of the young girls visiting the abortion clinics are children of parents in those very churches.

This is antithetical to the role of the church in

Scripture and runs completely counter to the history of American churches. Before there even was an "America," the churches of colonial America were so influential in urging their congregations to separate from England (an obviously political move) that many in Europe referred to the American Revolution as "The Presbyterian Rebellion." British Prime Minister Horace Walpole is said to have lamented to Parliament, "Cousin America has run off with a Presbyterian parson," referring to John Witherspoon, one of the signers of the Declaration of Independence. It wasn't the Presbyterian Church alone that urged the colonists to pledge their lives, their fortunes, and their sacred honor in pursuit of freedom; there were Congregationalist, Dutch Reformed, and Lutheran churches, to name just a few. However, their pastors were largely united in their understanding that the church was to be salt *and* light in the culture.

It is not enough to bring the light of God's truth about salvation through faith in Christ alone—as critically important as this message is. The church must also be *salt*. The church must come into contact with the culture, actually be *pressed into* the culture in order to do its proper preserving work. A church that separates and segregates itself from the culture is not acting in accordance with Scripture.

Historian David Barton often tells the stirring account of John Peter Muhlenberg, a Lutheran pastor who stood before his congregation and preached a sermon taken from Ecclesiastes 3:1-8. "In the language of Holy Writ, there is a time for all things," Muhlenberg told his flock. "There is a time to preach and a time to fight."[58] With that, he removed his clerical robes to reveal the uniform of a colonel in the Continental Army with which he served until the end of the war. These men knew nothing of a radical "separation of church and state." They read a Bible that commanded them to shine the light of God's truth into every aspect of life and to vigorously engage in the culture—even at the risk of their lives.

The notion that the church should remain silent on cultural and moral issues is a postmodern concept, and it is one that is destructive to society as a whole. A church that has been scared into abdicating its responsibility to be salt makes itself culturally irrelevant. Such churches, even though they may go out to evangelize and bring the light of God's truth to a nation of lost people, have essentially admitted that the "truth" they preach has no bearing on practical life and the affairs of government, finance, and education. This "truth" is only for addressing spiritual life, as if "practical" and "spiritual" are two separate realms. These churches are preaching a "half-gospel"—one that has been stripped of much of its biblical power and influence.

To be crystal clear: this surrender is completely foreign to a proper Christian worldview. Paul makes it clear in 2 Timothy 3:16-18 that the Christian believer is *thoroughly equipped for every good work* by his or her knowledge of Scripture. The Bible provides total truth for every aspect of life—not just those elements, such as prayer and the singing of hymns, that many have set aside for Sunday mornings.

Dr. D. James Kennedy, who spent forty-seven years encouraging and equipping Christians to engage the culture, once wrote:

> Christians need to drop the compartmentalized view of Christianity that has gripped so many in our culture today. We need to recognize that this is our Father's

world; He is its Lord, and we need to
redeem as much of it as we can while
there is yet time.... He Himself told
us to "occupy" until He comes (Luke
19:13, KJV).[59]

It is unhealthy for individuals, churches, and nations to
create this artificial fault line between the "the secular and
the sacred." There should be no such line.

Intimidation

Another way the MMD has influenced the church is
through intimidation. The MMD does not regard
Christians as just out-of-touch or fringe; increasingly
Christians are painted as dangerous extremists. The
MMD uses its power to silence the church because that
silence gives secular humanists permission to say and do
whatever they want. Twenty years ago the church was
largely ignored when it attempted to salt the culture with
Christian truth. Today, when Christians seek to enter into
"mainstream" media discourse, they are chastised for
trying to impose "religion" onto an unwilling populace.

Shortly after Coral Ridge Ministries announced plans
for our 2008 Truths that Transform America conference,
Americans United for Separation of Church and State
posted an article warning its readers that I was intent on
imposing my "rigid view of the Bible" on America, thus
"sullying the U.S. Constitution and running our lives."

The article correctly quoted me as saying, "It is a
pivotal, crucial time in the history of our country.... As it
was with so many other points in history, it is the church
that will be the determining factor on which course
America goes." The author then warned that I am "joining
forces with some of the most extreme voices of the

Religious Right movement." The article further suggested darkly that some in this "fringe" element favor the death penalty for children who curse their parents.[60]

A writer for another web blog for atheists drew an inaccurate and fearful conclusion. After reading one of our newsletters in which I quoted Jesus' words from Mark 9:42: "Whoever causes one of these little ones who believe to stumble, it would be better for him if, with a heavy millstone hung around his neck, he had been cast into the sea," the author warned that the CEO of Coral Ridge Ministries was suggesting that Christians should drown atheists.[61]

Hyperbole, sarcasm, and deception are common tools of people who are puppets of the MMD. While such attacks lack serious thought and reason, the intent to drive all Christian expression from the public square is very real. Nancy Pearcey, who co-authored *How Now Shall We Live?* with Charles Colson, warns Christians about "the cultural captivity of the gospel," which "traps Christianity in the upper story of privatized values, and prevents it from having any effect on public culture." In her book *Total Truth*, Pearcey quotes the late actor Christopher Reeves, who scolded Christians for weighing in on the stem cell debate. "When matters of public policy are debated," Reeves intoned, "no religions should have a seat at the table."[62]

Should your faith exclude you from participation in the determination of public policy? *San Francisco Chronicle* columnist Mark Morford thinks so. He has written that groups like Focus on the Family "have proven that they can be highly dangerous, utterly toxic to the culture as a whole. You already know the list—FCC crackdowns, stem cell research, ultraconservative judges, abstinence education, anti-choice laws, vicious homophobia, intelligent design, the rejection of science—all of which aim for the creation of a fascist theocracy in America."[63]

Other members of the Hollywood elite are even more shrill in declaring their views. Rosie O'Donnell, speaking as a co-host on the Emmy Award winning daytime talk show *The View*, opined that "Radical Christianity is just as threatening as radical Islam in a country like America." MSNBC news analyst, Jennifer Pozner, founder of an organization called "Women in the Media and News," has adamantly defended O'Donnell's remarks.[64]

This open hostility has a chilling effect. No one likes being compared to Al Qaeda, so perhaps the simplest way to avoid such attacks is to remain silent. The church has developed a virtual "glass jaw" in these areas. One little jab from the MMD sends the church reeling onto the ropes, bleeding and beaten. Many Christians have been intimidated into abdicating their biblical obligation to address the cultural issues of the day.

The irony of the claim that religion should be kept separate from all other aspects of life is that it is impossible to do so. I challenge you to find any person in America who forms his or her views about economics, government, finance, culture, the arts, education, war, or the value of life outside of a spiritual context. It is not possible. Our worldview shapes the context for all other judgments, and every worldview is ultimately based on our views of God, spirituality, the afterlife, our purpose, and our existence. We are what we believe.

Those who cry loudly for the separation of religion from the public square actually base that very cry on religious beliefs. Whether they are atheist or agnostic at heart, their rejection of God (itself a religious position) is at the core of their desire to see Him banned from community life. This highlights the double standard we face in our cultural engagement. Secular humanism, the idea that man is the measure of all things, is atheistic but has been recognized by the U.S. Supreme Court as a religion.[65] While the media of mass deception vigilantly guard the schoolhouse door against any religious intruders, they are happy to have the religion of secular humanism reign supreme inside the classrooms of America.

Don't be deceived—it is completely impossible to keep religion out of public life. Those who wish to separate the two are simply exhibiting the behavior we should expect from hearts that have rejected God. Hearts that reject God will attempt to push Him as far away from their own lives as possible—even using intimidation to do so.

The Almighty Dollar

There is a practical reason why the Church has been struggling to act as salt in our media culture—it's expensive. For years the highly centralized structure of the MMD has made the media realm too costly for Christian artists, newsmakers, producers, and teachers to gain a solid foothold. Based on my professional experience in Christian radio, I will use the music industry as an example.

As mentioned earlier, by the 1980s Christian music artists recorded for Christian record labels. These labels, by and large, lagged behind their secular counterparts in terms of quality, distribution, and sales. The Christian labels were struggling to gain traction because this fledgling industry was trying to compete with music empires like Sony and Capitol Records. They didn't have the dollars or the distribution to compete. Then we saw the phenomenon of the so-called "crossover artists," such

81

as Michael W. Smith, Amy Grant, dc Talk, and the Winans. They began to get hits on secular radio. Many readers will recall the tremendous success that Christian artist Bob Carlisle had in 1997 with the song "Butterfly Kisses," a song still played at weddings across America.

As the executives of the major record labels recognized the potential for marketing explicitly Christian material, most Christian music companies were bought out by the larger and more powerful secular music companies. I was one of the few who welcomed these buyouts—it meant better marketing, better quality, and better distribution of Christian worldview music into a culture that desperately needed music proclaiming the hope and salvation of Jesus Christ.

The takeover of Christian labels by secular companies was by no means perfect. There is a greater possibility the theology of Christian music will be watered down when secular companies have control. But the opportunity to invest more money in the production and distribution of Christian music is exponentially increased.

I hope Christian music continues to make progress in influencing the culture. Today it still remains somewhat segregated from other forms of music. We can and should pray that God will raise up Christian artists and producers who will develop and create music that speaks just as powerfully to the culture as it did some fifty or sixty years ago. We should pray for music that appeals to the mainstream and glorifies God at the same time. We should pray that once again the Christian worldview would be the foundation for popular music—not a separate genre.

The secular media empire operates within a high-cost structure, which forces Christian media outlets into exceptionally small distribution channels so that they have to struggle to make an impact on the culture. In addition to this challenge, the secular media empires are for-profit corporations. Many of the Christian media organizations are non-profit. Americans view and support for-profits and non-profits differently.

Coral Ridge Ministries provides a good example of the challenges of meeting the high costs of media distribution. We have been producing a television program and radio broadcasts since the 1970s. Through the years, our goal has been to use high impact media to proclaim biblical truths that will produce personal and cultural transformation through the inspiration of the Holy Spirit. We strive to provide our audiences with the scriptural grounding they need to make intelligent judgments about the major cultural issues of the day. The millions of ministry partners who have remained faithful to us for more than three decades, plus the swelling numbers of newcomers to our broadcast ministries, are proof positive that we are providing an important service to the Christian community. We broadcast on several hundred TV and radio stations in this country and around the world.

The costs associated with producing and distributing these programs are very high. Over half of our operating budget goes to produce and market the TV and radio outreaches. The rest of the budget is used to develop curricula, print books and materials, support and develop Internet outreaches, maintain technology, provide salaries for our staff, raise funds, and pay for operating costs. We reach an audience of approximately three million people with Christian truth, and we pray that number is growing.

However, the American population demands quality, quantity, and entertainment from its media. Billion-dollar corporations can fill that need because they have the investment capital available for production and advertising.

Non-profit media ministries like CRM are funded (at least in our case) largely through donations from the public. The very largest non-profits in America are not media organizations; they are relief or charitable ministries. The handful of worldwide non-profit media ministries do not compare in size and scope with the multi-billion dollar TV conglomerates.

In the ultra competitive and costly realm of TV and radio, the "Golden Rule" applies—he who has the gold makes the rules. In the world of media, the availability of funds makes an enormous difference in the quality and reach of the programming offered to the public.

Letters of thanks pour in from listeners and viewers all over the nation who have been impacted by the Word of God through Coral Ridge Ministries. However, the expense of producing high quality media makes it difficult for smaller organizations, such as CRM, to compete with the humanistic messages of the media of mass deception, which run on large budgets stemming from advertising and investing dollars. For example, ABC invests millions into producing immoral shows like *Desperate Housewives*,[66] which is watched weekly in nearly twenty million homes.[67]

This "he who has the gold makes the rules" pattern has repeated itself in virtually every major media venue, *with the exception of the Internet*. Christian-themed movies are created with budgets that are usually a fraction of the major releases, and many have stumbled badly at the box office, due to lack of marketing and advertising support. There are large Christian television programmers, such as the Trinity Broadcasting Network and the Inspiration Network, but they are dwarfed by the Big Three networks and the major cable networks. Their programming is developed to appeal specifically to Christian viewers, so it often fails to capture the attention of a broader audience. Because most Christian media organizations are non-profits, both investing and advertising dollars are not available.

Nevertheless, there is some good news here: Despite the long history of humanistic dominance in TV and movies, the winds of change are stirring. Not only are Christian movies making a much bigger impact today than before, many of the controlling companies in media today are opening up divisions to create content for a Christian worldview audience. These include Fox Faith (*End of the Spear*) and Sony Provident-Integrity (*The Gospel, The Second Chance*). Walt Disney Company, the object of a years-long boycott by the American Family Association, the Southern Baptist Convention, and the Catholic League, has announced that it plans to place greater emphasis on family-friendly films.[68] We can only hope that as large corporations produce movies and shows set within a biblical moral framework, our culture will respond by affirming this type of programming.

The recent history of the publishing industry is a bit more complicated than that of the music and film industries. The Bible is not only the best-selling book of all time; it also continues to be the best-selling book every year. Annual sales of the Bible are estimated at half a *billion* dollars.[69] With such a reliable anchor seller, a number of Christian publishers have flourished for years, including industry heavyweights such as Thomas Nelson, Zondervan, and Tyndale. Yet the books they publish are ignored or dismissed by the media of mass deception.

However, more and more of the secular giants, like their counterparts in music, are recognizing that there is plenty of money to be made selling books to Christians. Tyndale House Publishers released the *Left Behind* series, and the publishing world changed dramatically. Sixty-five million book sales and seven *New York Times* #1 best-sellers later,[70] it was obvious that there is a huge market for well-written Christian fiction. Publishers scrambled to get into the game, and found that there is a market for more than Christian fiction. Bruce Wilkinson's *The Prayer of Jabez* sold nine million copies in two years,[71] and Rick Warren's *The Purpose Driven Life* is the best-selling non-fiction hardcover in publishing history.[72]

But where does the money from all those book sales go? The profits flow into the publicly owned firms that own the MMD. These major media empires have the dollars to spend on advertising and distribution that allow them to capture the hearts and minds of Americans. It has been extremely difficult, if not impossible, for small, innovative Christian media companies to break into an arena that is dominated by multi-billion dollar for-profit companies. It is almost as if the best that these small companies can hope for is to attract enough attention from the "big boys" to sell out at a reasonable profit. The high costs of producing and distributing media have posed a huge challenge to the church at large.

Stocking the Life Boats

When the church abandoned its biblical responsibility to provide moral leadership in the culture, the media of mass deception rushed in to fill the vacuum. Decades later the MMD is fiercely protective of what it has marked out as its territory. It has attempted to keep Christians silent by means of the eight tactics previously mentioned. In addition, the major media empires have succeeded in keeping Christians relegated to small markets, because they have far more dollars to work with. Just as the problem of cultural disengagement grew sharply worse with the church in the 1960s, it is continuing with the twenty-first century church, which, to a large extent, has developed a defeatist outlook.

Eschatology is the word that theologians use for "the study of last things," or "the end times." Eschatology seeks to interpret the Bible's teaching about the second coming of Christ and the establishment of His eternal kingdom. The American church has widely adopted a view of eschatology which essentially teaches that life on earth will grow increasingly distressing, filled with famine, war, and natural disasters. Jesus will then come and rapture His church just before things get *really* unpleasant. The result of this understanding of the end times is that a good portion of the American church seems to be resigned to the "certainty" that American culture will decline and violence will increase.

This view inculcates the gravely dangerous attitude that the *Titanic* is sinking and there is nothing we can do to stop it. The luxury liner of American culture has struck an iceberg and has torn an irreparable gash in its side. It is only a matter of time before the entire structure will slowly but surely disappear into the dark, cold waters of sin, corruption, and relativism. So we must pray that Jesus will come quickly to save us from a sure and terrible fate. As a result of this belief, many in the church retreat and just wait for the end to come.

I am not a seminarian, and I certainly didn't write *Media Revolution* to make a definitive statement on eschatology, but I do know this: whatever our eschatological position, it should not prevent us from obeying Christ's command to be salt and light. Our end times perspective should have no bearing on the amount of time and energy we put into bringing Christ into every facet of our existence. To assume that the church can have only a modest effect on the popular culture is to deny the power of the gospel and God's Word.

A Christian should be an eternal optimist. Can America be turned around morally, culturally, politically, legally, and socially? Without a doubt! Can the media be reformed to where it conveys truth, biblical wisdom, and a Christian worldview? Yes, most certainly. Can we return to being the world's bastion of Christianity—a place where peace, security, justice, and compassion abound? No question about it. Do you think our culture is too far gone to reform? Then consider the example of William Wilberforce and other British evangelicals who brought moral reform to their nation in the nineteenth century.

One Man Can Make a Difference

Wilberforce, a member of Parliament from 1780 to 1824, set for himself two goals. One was to end the British slave trade. The other was to reform British morals, which were deplorably base in the late eighteenth century. With the help of others, he largely succeeded. The slave trade was abolished in 1807 and in 1833, just three days before his death, Parliament abolished slavery—an act that brought freedom to some 800,000 slaves.

Wilberforce saw similar success in his moral crusade. Wilberforce biographer John Pollock writes that "the essentials of his beliefs and of his conscience formed the foundation of the British character for the next two generations at least. He was a proof that a man may change his times, though he cannot do it alone."[73]

The historical example of Wilberforce provides a tremendous lesson. The social change that he and others achieved can happen again. His life offers stirring documentation for the claim that believers in Jesus Christ can bring moral renewal to a culture. Politics is not the only arena in which moral change can be effected, of course. It is first and foremost the Gospel of Jesus Christ that transforms our hearts and creates the foundation from which change comes to individuals, families, and cultures. When we salt the culture with a biblical moral witness and light up the darkness with the message of Christ, enormous change can and will take place.

In a riveting sermon preached to his congregation at Coral Ridge Presbyterian Church, Dr. D. James Kennedy implored his flock to be active in every sphere—evangelizing the lost and engaging in the great cultural issues of the day. I'm told his thundering voice softened into a whisper as he concluded:

> Ah, dear one, Christ wants you to be a soldier for Him. Pray that God will fill you with intensity to do whatever you can, to become involved, to get out of the bleachers and onto the field and become a participant in the greatest struggle in the history of the world—a struggle for goodness, a struggle for godliness, a struggle of Christ against Satan. That is the battle we are in.[74]

Scripture commands Christians to be busy doing our Master's work. Christ is Lord of all, and we are to be stewards of all He has given us. There are those who believe that our only response to cultural decay is to preach the gospel of salvation. We should indeed be preaching salvation, but that is just providing the "light" and not spreading the "salt."

Be Careful Little Eyes What You See

A second, more prosaic reason for the existence of a defeatist attitude in the church is that many Christians believe that what they see on television is "normal." In fact, we must realize that the television broadcast blitz is overwhelmingly negative. Virtually all primetime dramas deal with murder and violence—with a large dose of illicit sex thrown in for good measure. If you tune in to the nightly news, you are showered with more bloodshed, more rape, and more murder. "If it bleeds, it leads," is the conventional wisdom on the television news.

This media bombardment of crashes and carnage leads to a highly skewed picture of America. The reality is that the United States is in far better shape than the MMD shows, because television does *not* reflect reality. What we see on our televisions is there because it sells advertising. The top news anchors are celebrities, first and foremost— their annual salaries run into the tens of millions of dollars. Stories are sensationalized and bad news is exaggerated, all done to take advantage of our natural tendency to slow down and stare when we see a wreck on the highway. The networks' primary job is to secure ratings, because ratings sell advertising and advertising is what keeps the networks in business. Always remember that network news and programming are not designed or intended to be truthful—they are designed to attract viewers, because with viewers comes money.

For more than twenty years, Michael Eisner was the CEO of the Walt Disney Company, which owns ABC and ESPN. Shortly before leaving Paramount Pictures to join Disney, Eisner wrote, "We have no obligation to make history. We have no obligation to make art. We have no obligation to make a statement. To make money is our only objective."[75] Roy Disney (nephew of the late Walt Disney) accused Eisner of turning Disney into a "rapacious, soulless" company.[76]

Sterling Rome worked as an assistant to Walter Cronkite, the dean of network news anchors. Mr. Rome succinctly explains the change that took place in news reporting near the close of the twentieth century:

> Back in the "golden age" of television, news divisions were the unprofitable badges of honor worn by the networks to provide prestige (and cover) from public criticism. The networks would point to their distinguished news bureaus as proof that they deserved the public trust and access to the airwaves the government had given them free of charge.
>
> But with the arrival of local network news, competition became fierce, and "news" was bastardized to include accident reporting—segments on fires, car wrecks, random violence and any other titillating visuals that could be shot live on tape. Local news accident reporting was inexpensive and highly profitable—two things the national news, at that time, was not....
>
> When television began, news broadcasts were never required to be entertaining, only accurate. By stressing the value of "story" over the value of information, network news began the inevitable descent into biased reporting. Untethered

> from the facts, the character of a story
> becomes more reliant on the storyteller.[77]

The final sentence is chilling. "Untethered from the facts…." The six o'clock news will continue to broadcast as much negative, heart-wrenching, sensational news as possible, because the producers of these shows have no desire to inform the public. Their goal is to entertain their viewers, because that increases the size of their audience, which in turn increases the value of their parent companies' stock.

When Americans are inundated with bad news, day in and day out, it becomes very difficult to maintain a positive outlook. Our worldview is no longer shaped by biblical truth, but by the death, destruction, and sorrow beamed into our homes throughout the 24-hour news and programming cycle. We become fearful and threatened. We become wary and pessimistic, because of what we now perceive to be "normal."

Financial News: Nearly All "Bunk"

This principle also exists in the financial services sector, where I worked for several years. During this time I had ample opportunity to peer under the hood and see how that industry actually works. The parts of the financial services industry that are glitzy and glamorous are, in many ways, built on a web of lies. If you watch most financial shows on cable news channels, you will see programming with one core purpose: to attract more viewers. Fancy sets, fast-talking hosts, stocks of the day, trading tips, and lots of charts make the show appealing. The sole purpose of these broadcasts is to induce us to tune breathlessly in to the *next* show. "Appealing" and "practical" often mean two entirely different things.

Many of these shows encourage us to trade stocks more, time the market, pick the next hot investment, move funds, and overall develop a very short-term outlook to investing. Keep in mind that many brokerage firms advertise on these shows. How do these firms make their money? The more you trade your investments, the more money the brokerage makes. Do you think they are motivated to encourage us to be "proactive" in managing our money? True solid investing is based on long-term principles—and that bores some Americans.

A caricature of what it means to be an investor has been created. It is one that bears little resemblance to the vast majority of the American population, but it's sexy; it sells advertising, and that sells stock.

A few years ago I had lunch with John Bogle, creator of the modern index mutual fund, founder of Vanguard Investments, and one of the most respected investment minds of the twentieth century. He pioneered low cost, low activity investing for the common man. Vanguard is one of the world's largest and most successful mutual fund companies. During the course of our conversation, I asked him about the financial news on television and in print. I told him I thought 99 percent of the investing information provided through the media was bunk. He replied, "Ninety-nine percent? One hundred percent! I look at my own personal accounts maybe once a year." That type of investment philosophy doesn't make for exciting media coverage, so you rarely hear about it in the press.

Yet for all the talk you hear among Christians about their distrust of the media, we continue to watch these "news" shows night after night, and we begin to believe that what we are watching is a true representation of reality. We become convinced, sometimes at a subconscious level, that we are watching Truth and that the world is hurtling down the road to Armageddon. We see hate crimes legislation written to outlaw the preaching of Scripture; we see the Ten Commandments being removed from another government building; we see the yellow tape strung around a body lying under a sheet; and we begin to think that in just a few short years we'll be living in the Roman Empire, where Christians will be flayed and eaten by lions in the Coliseum.

I'm not saying that American life doesn't have its challenges and isn't in a state of decay. What I am saying is that we have the choice of how we view the situation. We can view it as an inevitable path toward destruction, or a wonderful opportunity to share life and culture-changing truth with an end result of peace, prosperity, and decency.

"Your Attitude Determines Your Altitude"

Whether from bad theology, bad news, or both, Christians have developed a pessimistic attitude and have, to a large degree, withdrawn from the culture. A few of us evangelize; many of us don't. Many have abandoned any idea that we should be salt in the culture. This is foolishness. There are millions all around us in desperate need of a Savior and sound biblical wisdom. The harvest is plentiful and the workers are few. Let us increase the number of the workers!

There is a passage of Scripture that summarizes the church's role in the culture. In his epistle to Titus, Paul wrote to his "true son in our common faith" to give him instructions on how to build and strengthen the church. Included are these words:

> For the grace of God has appeared,

bringing salvation to all men, instructing us to deny ungodliness and worldly desires and to live sensibly, righteously and godly in the present age, looking for the blessed hope and the appearing of the glory of our great God and Savior, Christ Jesus, who gave Himself for us to redeem us from every lawless deed, and to purify for Himself a people for His own possession, zealous for good deeds. These things speak and exhort and reprove with all authority. Let no one disregard you (Titus 2:11-15).

Paul told Titus to look forward to the blessed hope of the second coming of Christ. *But that wasn't all he said.* We are to be "zealous for good deeds." I don't see anything about retreating from the culture in those words. We are to "speak…exhort, and reprove," without shrinking back from the verbal barbs launched at us by those who disagree. We are to let our light shine before men in such a way that they may see our good works and glorify our Father who is in heaven. (Matthew 5:16). All of this is included in *engaging with* the culture. We are not to retreat from it. As salt was pressed into meat to keep it from spoiling, we must act as a preservative for our society by fearlessly and innovatively presenting God's truth in the marketplace of ideas.

If you have already decided that America cannot be turned around, I strongly urge you to reconsider your position in light of Scripture. God blesses a pure heart and real repentance. He has promised repeatedly that if we turn from our wicked ways and repent, He will bless us. If you believe that God's judgment will fall on America for its decades of sin and immorality, you may well be right. But God is also a patient God, a loving God, and a just God. He honors even the smallest and weakest among us who repents, prays, and obeys.

If you have been thinking that what we all see on the news reflects the vast majority view of American culture, remember this: the media of mass deception exists to make money. It no longer cares about truth, facts, reality, or its impact on you. It cares about accumulating new listeners, readers, and viewers so that it can continue to attract advertising dollars. At the end of the day, the MMD wants to be able to charge top dollar to those who wish to get their message to you. The truthfulness of the message is irrelevant.

Don't be a pawn or a victim. The media revolution is about the church in America shaking off the deception and bringing God's absolute truth to bear in a culture that desperately needs it. Become a part of the solution; don't continue to be a part of the problem. The remainder of this book will show you how.

PART TWO

JOIN THE REVOLUTION!

4

THE DEMOCRATIZATION OF AMERICAN MEDIA

I stated in the introduction that the media of mass deception is slowly but surely losing its ability to influence our nation. The evidence of this deconstruction is seen in four different mediums: television, radio, print, and the Internet. Overall, we are seeing what I call the "democratization" of American media—the power of the media is being seized from a few large, dictatorial conglomerates and being given back to individuals. This is the heart of the *Media Revolution*. Common people—people like you and me—now can have tremendous control over media.

Consider this point: If the majority of people hold a Christian worldview in whole or in part (Gallup reports that about 80% of Americans claim to be Christian[78]) and media influence is being handed to these masses of people, we are about to see a monumental shift in the content and purpose of the media. Here is the most important point of this book—*you can help make that happen!*

As people with a Christian worldview begin to have far more influence in and through media, the overall message of the media will change. Instead of being a dominant machine that pours out deception onto the helpless American people, the new media will become a powerful influence for truth. As millions of people gain a voice in the culture, foundational values and principles long relegated to the cultural backwaters will once again be a part of the main tide of our culture and will begin touching and transforming the lives of many Americans who have been lied to for so long. The Word of God does not return void. The truth of it still sets men and women free. We now have the opportunity to use the media to transform America back into a country that is standing strong on its godly Christian heritage.

I believe that the MMD was at the heart of the decline in American culture, principles, and values that began over 50 years ago. Its effects have been felt in all areas of life, including politics, education, religious life, the arts, local and national security, and economics. I also believe that a truthful revolution in media will, in time, be the impetus for positive change in those same areas. Media leads the way—whether it be into deception or truth, in decay or growth, negativism or optimism, godlessness or godliness.

What is making it possible for Americans to take such a powerful foothold in the media is a collapse of an entrenched media establishment, which has controlled the messages and viewpoints of this nation for decades. These older empires are being replaced by new media, led by Internet and related technologies. This collapse is occurring because of the combination of several factors, most notably the incredible rise of the Internet and its far-reaching effects on virtually all aspects of life. Other factors include competition in cable and satellite TV, the return of FM and AM talk radio, the change in advertising trends, and shifts in cultural preferences. Although the technical reasons for this reconstruction of the media are beyond the scope of this book, suffice it to say that the Internet is causing a profoundly sweeping change in TV, radio, and print communications. A revolution is underway.

The Coming Decline of the MMD

Several manifestations of the decline of the MMD are evident in the major television networks. The first indication is cable television's reach into the vast majority of American homes, coupled with the rapid growth of satellite television. With the exponential increase in the number of channels available, the viewing habits of the American population have become diversified. CNN, MTV, and ESPN were some of the most notable niche market pioneers responsible for this divergence. Today, music and movie channels, soap opera channels, game show channels, cartoon channels, and educational television all make up part of the ever-expanding palette of viewing options available to the American public. There has been steady erosion in the market share of the Big Three networks, which formerly enjoyed a decades-long monopoly over what our nation saw and consumed.

In recent years the Internet has exploded onto the consciousness of the American public, drawing a huge share of advertising dollars away from television to this burgeoning new field, which remains a largely unregulated medium. A phenomenal historic opportunity exists for the American public to exert its influence once again on the media through the Internet and related technologies.

Radio has also undergone dramatic transformation. Satellite radio is still in its infancy, but we can be certain it will continue to grow. FM radio had pushed the AM radio market close to extinction, but then came the emergence of talk radio. It has been said that Rush Limbaugh single-handedly saved AM radio, and that is probably not hyperbole. AM radio has profitably settled into news-talk, sports-talk, specialty, and ethnic broadcasting niches. FM radio has maintained its emphasis on music and conceded some of the talk format to AM.

Once again the ubiquity of the Internet is factoring into the radio equation. A fascinating synergy is developing between radio and Internet. An example can be found in the radio ministry of John Piper, the influential Reformed Baptist pastor from Minnesota. He recently decided to pull all his broadcasts from terrestrial radio stations and now broadcasts exclusively over the Internet—and he is finding great success.

Surprisingly, there is even an impressive revolution taking place in the publishing industry, which is one of the mediums most resistant to change. Traditionally, publishers have exerted tremendous control over what books are printed and put to market. They have had confidence that their books would be received and purchased by the reading public through standard outlets. Today, some are scrambling to figure out how to remain profitable. Most major publishers have narrowed their focus and directed their resources toward a handful of authors and projects that have the highest profit potential.

Once again, the Internet is largely responsible for this transformation. Amazon.com played a large role in the diversification of the distribution arm of the publishing industry by bringing book buyers online. The cost of publishing books has decreased, thanks to the new print on demand (POD) technology, which allows virtually anyone to self-publish his or her own book. Distribution and inventory costs used to make publishing your own book a financially challenging venture; today you can invest a few hundred dollars, stimulate demand by marketing your book on the Internet, and get surprisingly good results.

I produced a book in 2002 without shopping it to a single major publisher. I wrote *Seven Investment Tales* and sent it off to an independent publishing/printing company. A friend of mine did the layout, art, and graphics on his home computer. I was able to print a few thousand copies for $2.50 a book. Marketing the book was simple. It was placed on Amazon.com, in a few local bookstores, and sold live at events where I spoke. My costs were covered and I had a profitable project within a year.

This kind of self-publishing was all but unheard of ten or fifteen years ago. Was my book a *New York Times* bestseller? No—but it served its purpose, and here is a very important factor for those of us who enjoy writing books: I never lost the ownership rights. No one else was able to control the production or distribution of the book. Having heard far too many stories of how authors and musicians write original material only to cede contractual control to a publishing company that can then market and distribute the work however it wants, I find it fascinating that the power of this industry is truly returning to the people.

Another development in the publishing industry is paperless technology. Audio books have been slowly but steadily growing in popularity, and the Internet now allows readers to download books to personal computers and even handheld devices. While many of us love having an actual book to hold and pages to turn, other readers place much less importance on the "look, feel, and smell" of an actual book and enjoy reading on their computers.

All of these developments mean that the culture is moving away from having one or two sources of information and is expanding to an array of multiple choices. I am just one example of millions of people who take advantage of this competitive environment. I rarely watch network news or cable news channels and I don't read the local newspapers. But every day I go to three or four different Internet websites to check the news throughout the day. I regularly read books by authors who are commenting on current issues and also download podcasts of short audio news clips. Frequently I read blogs by authors I trust and respect to gain insight and information. The bottom line for me is that I regularly check between four and six different sources of news and information—none of which are provided or controlled by the Big Three television networks or a deceptive national press.

The Cheap Revolution

Several years ago I heard Rich Karlgaard of *Forbes* magazine speaking about what he called "the cheap revolution." The cheap revolution occurs when industries experience a significant decrease in the cost to deliver a product or service due to some technological advancement. He gave several examples, such as the cellular phone industry that was available only to the very wealthy fifteen years ago. Today you can get your cell phone for free. It is quite conceivable that within this decade, cell phones may enjoy the same kind of market penetration as radio. We have seen the same phenomenon occur with personal computers, televisions, software, and media players.

The media industry is also being heavily impacted by the cheap revolution. Ten years ago it was unheard of for someone to own a top quality camera that could be used to produce a reasonable television broadcast or movie. Today you buy a webcam for under $100 and 100,000 people are watching your video on YouTube.com inside of a half-hour. I recently checked out a video on GodTube.com of a cute little girl reciting Psalm 23 from memory. That video has received over 4.8 million views, more than many network television shows. What did it take to produce it? Just one webcam, one computer, one proud dad, and one very charming and smart little girl.

The music industry has been similarly impacted. In 1990, if you wanted to make a record, you had to go to one of the major recording studios in Los Angeles, Miami, Nashville, or New York. If you tried to record something on your own, you were immediately at a disadvantage. The equipment to produce such an album was prohibitively expensive. Even if you could afford to record it, you had to find a way to distribute it. Just ten years later, with a personal computer and a $1,000 software package, you can put in a little work and produce something of exceptional quality. Distributing your album has become far more economical and easier because of downloadable music on the Internet. Today, because of the cheap revolution that has occurred in the music industry, bands can bypass the traditional gatekeepers of the music industry and produce excellent work in a garage or living room. Is this movement a major force in the music industry? Not yet, but it's coming.

5

IS IT POSSIBLE?

There are a number of excellent books that outline how the media in America became increasingly secularized and humanistic—a process that accelerated between the 1950s and the 1970s. There are good books that demonstrate how a small minority of powerful people own the vast majority of the media outlets and how they have used those outlets to disseminate their messages. While preparing to write this book, I was struck by the fact that few of these authors present a specific plan to change the current situation. As I said at the outset, one of the core purposes of this book is to present a *plan* for us, as Christians, to bring Christ and a biblical worldview back into the mainstream culture through media.

Imagine with me for a moment an America where biblical creation is taught widely in the public schools. Imagine that the killing of the unborn is illegal again, that we would value human life so highly that the very thought of abortion or euthanasia is repugnant. Imagine school administrators objecting that there isn't *enough* prayer in schools and no one is questioning celebrating Christ at Christmas. Think about what our nation will be like if marriage between a man and a woman were to be honored for its biblical heritage and recognized far and wide as the core foundation of our society. Imagine an America where the Christian worldview is the dominant worldview in politics, economics, culture, art, finance, history, law, and healthcare. What would our culture look like then?

I have just outlined the ACLU's worst nightmare. Some critics of this book will call it unrealistic and antiquated. They will probably say that I am trying to lead Americans on a path back to the unenlightened stone ages. I will respond in advance: If a society that honors God; cherishes life; teaches the phenomenal fact that we can spend eternity in heaven; protects personal property; has a government that promotes itself less, not more; obeys the Golden Rule; and upholds marriage, liberty, decency, and morality is called "the stone age," call me a caveman. But if we are to believe the polls and statistics about mainstream America, what I have just outlined is what the vast majority of Americans truly desire. They want a society of peace, true justice, transparency, and purity.

You may view this vision for America with great skepticism, believing that America has traveled too far down a road from which there is no turning back. I have heard scores of reasons why America cannot return to a culture that honors God and weaves His Word into the very fabric of our culture. But there is one reason why it is very, very possible: God honors a people who honor Him. The Sovereign Lord has promised, "[If] My people who are called by My name humble themselves, and pray and seek My face, and turn from their wicked ways, then I will hear from heaven, will forgive their sin and heal their land" (2 Chronicles 7:14). Therefore, we must, as Cardinal Francis J. Spellman said so well, "Pray as if everything depended on God, and work as if everything depended upon man."

After being reduced to chomping on grass like a cow, King Nebuchadnezzar said:

> I lifted my eyes to heaven, and my reason returned to me, and I blessed the Most High, and praised and honored him who lives forever, for his dominion is an everlasting dominion, and his kingdom endures from generation to generation; all the inhabitants of the earth are accounted as nothing, and he does according to his will among the host of heaven and among the inhabitants of the earth; and none can stay his hand or say to him, "What have you done?" (Daniel 4:34-35 ESV).

God can and will do exactly as He pleases with the inhabitants of the earth, and if we humble ourselves and turn from our sinful, defeatist, self-centered lifestyles and live lives that give praise and honor to Him who lives forever, He has *promised* to heal our land. We must pray without ceasing, knowing with utter certainty that unless the Spirit of the Sovereign Lord sweeps across this land, there is no other prescription for America. We must pray that reason returns to this nation.

But when we arise from our prayers, we must work. God has instructed us to trust in Him with all our hearts, to acknowledge Him in all our ways, and to *work* to bring His name to the world. And one of the most important works to be done in reforming our culture is to reform the media that feeds it information.

A Christian Worldview

Before I lay out the battle plan for using the media to bring the Christian worldview back to the American people, let's take a few moments to sketch what we are referring to when we speak of a "Christian worldview." We do not have space for an elaborate explanation here, and so if you want to investigate this subject in greater depth, I would recommend that you read some of the works cited in this section.[79] But it will be helpful for us to provide a context here for our discussions later.

In *How Now Shall We Live?*, Charles Colson and Nancy Pearcey state that every worldview provides an answer for three basic questions:

- Where did we come from, and who are we?
- What has gone wrong with the world?
- What can we do to fix it?

"These three questions," they explain, "form a grid that we can use to break down the inner logic of every belief system or philosophy we encounter, from the textbooks in our classrooms to the unspoken philosophy that shapes the message we hear on *Oprah*."[80] As Colson and Pearcey point out, "The basis for the Christian worldview, of course, is God's revelation in Scripture.... Scripture is intended to be the basis of all of life."[81]

David Noebel, in his comprehensive worldview study, *Understanding the Times*, cites Scottish theologian James Orr as a pioneer in articulating the ramifications of a Christian worldview. We can borrow from Orr's definitions[82] to answer the three questions presented by Colson and Pearcey:

Where did we come from, and who are we? All men are created in the image of God, and thus *all* human life, from the embryo to the elderly and infirm, is uniquely endowed with great dignity and value.

What has gone wrong with the world? Beginning with Adam's sin in the Garden of Eden, man has wickedly rebelled against God and His commands for life and happiness. Adam's original sin in the Garden is known as "the fall," and our continued rebellion is known as "sin." Sin has so corrupted our every faculty that we are incapable, apart from the gracious work of the Holy Spirit, to think or act in a wise or godly manner.

What can we do to fix it? God's gracious purpose for the salvation of sinful mankind centers in the Person and work of Jesus Christ, God's only Son, who is the new Head of humanity. The redemption of sinful human beings was accomplished through Christ's atoning death on the cross. This salvation is appropriated by faith, and by faith alone; those who place their trust in Jesus Christ will not perish, but have eternal life (John 3:16).

But "fixing" the world doesn't stop here. The Bible—God's inspired, infallible, inerrant Word—is the revelation of all truth and provides us with God's commands for how we are to live. Scripture describes the creation of the world by God; His immanent presence in it; and His sovereign, holy, and wise government of the world for His perfect purpose.

Scripture also declares that Jesus Christ has established a Kingdom of God on earth—a kingdom which includes not only the spiritual salvation of individuals, but spiritual principles for ordering society. Christ's followers are commanded to expend every effort to proclaim the gospel and to develop a culture that honors and exalts Christ and His Word. Our efforts to do so should spring forth from a life of grateful service.

D. James Kennedy and Jerry Newcombe authored the book *Lord of All* to encourage and equip Christians to live lives of grateful service by being engaged in the "six great spheres that every Christian should be vitally interested in and should be working to Christianize."[83] These spheres are: 1) the world, 2) humanity, 3) the nation, 4) the school, 5) the church, and 6) the family. These are the areas every individual believer and every Christian church should be seeking to influence with the truth of Scripture and the love of Christ. The Christian worldview proclaims that the Triune God is sovereign over every aspect of life, and therefore His Word and His principles should guide us in each of these areas of human society.

Standing in stark contrast to the Christian worldview is the dominant worldview of the media of mass deception—naturalism. The Christian worldview declares, "In the beginning God created the heavens and the earth" (Genesis 1:1). Naturalism asserts, "There is no God and there can be no supernatural explanation for the origin of the human race. Everything that exists finds its origins in the impersonal forces of nature, as observed and explained by science."

A naturalistic worldview might be expressed in the following ways:

Where did we come from, and who are we? Naturalists insist that we have emerged from the primordial soup and evolved over billions of years. American schoolchildren are taught that they are the direct descendants of apes. Dr. Kennedy and Jerry Newcombe observed that the naturalist would say that we are "the product of time and slime."[84]

What has gone wrong with the world? A naturalist would explain that racism and religious bigotry have kept civilizations from reaching their full potential. Man's religious superstitions have caused him to reject the wisdom of science and philosophy. As a result, according to naturalism, instead of moving towards greater enlightenment and world peace, men continue to battle and enslave one another.

What can we do to fix it? The naturalistic worldview rejects all religion, particularly Christianity. It would have us embrace its own "scientific naturalism." Humanity will be improved by creating the right social and economic conditions. Naturalists place great emphasis on education and government (particularly world government) as the best solutions to mankind's problems. Furthermore, since there is no God, according to the naturalist, there are no moral absolutes. Therefore, we can and should do whatever feels right to us, so long as our actions don't interfere with "the greater good of society." That "greater good," of course, can only be properly defined by those who embrace naturalism.

Chuck Colson and Nancy Pearcey warn that this clash between the Christian and the naturalistic worldviews is "the root of our cultural crisis."[85] The promotion of naturalism in the media of mass deception has been so prevalent that many cultural observers have begun to describe the United States as a "post-Christian" nation. Many well-meaning Christians have succumbed to naturalistic worldview principles, mixing them with a Christian view. This not only weakens the church and waters down our faith, but it is also inherently destructive to the individual.

In a speech delivered more than twenty years before the outbreak of the Civil War, Abraham Lincoln asked rhetorically:

> Shall we expect some transatlantic military giant, to step the Ocean, and crush us at a blow? Never! All the armies of Europe, Asia and Africa combined, with all the treasure of the earth (our own excepted) in their military chest; with a Bonaparte for a commander, could not by force, take a drink from the Ohio, or make a track on the Blue Ridge, in a Trial of a thousand years.

> At what point then is the approach of danger to be expected? I answer, if it ever reach us, it must spring up amongst us. It cannot come from abroad. If destruction

be our lot, we must ourselves be its author and finisher. As a nation of freemen, we must live through all time, or die by suicide.[86]

If we heed the call of the naturalists to abandon our faith in God and His Word, we will commit national suicide. Currently, our nation is exposed to mass media outlets that are promoting that final, self-inflicted wound. We have been blitzed with messages from an anti-Christian media, yet, despite the best efforts of the MMD, the vast majority of Americans cling tenaciously to their faith in the God of the Bible. Recent polls show that some 90% of Americans believe in God[87] and 75% of our countrymen believe that the Bible's account of the death, burial, and resurrection of Jesus Christ is literally true.[88] It is a fact that the vast majority of Americans hold to some semblance of a Christian worldview. Is it perfect? Most definitely not. Can media be used to help us think more consistently with the Scriptures? Most definitely yes. Next we will consider some of the specific ways we can use media to do just that.

6

INNOVATION

The remainder of this book outlines a four-part plan for media transformation. Stated simply it involves:

- Innovation
- Intelligence
- Information
- Infiltration

This plan *will* work, but the church must decide that it *wants* it to work. The church must make a conscious decision to abandon its defeatist attitude and develop a genuine desire to reengage with the media of mass deception. Let's turn it into a media of mass revelation, transforming it into a megaphone for truth, goodness, and beauty. The church must decide that the Internet is a fertile ground for ministry and seek to use it, not solely for purposes of evangelization (although that's vital), but also to teach and proclaim biblical absolute truth as it applies to every aspect of life.

It is just that simple, and yet, just that eternally significant. Christians must determine to be optimistic; they must follow the mandates of Scripture accordingly; they must pray the Lord's Prayer *and believe it to be true*— "Thy kingdom come, thy will be done on earth as it is in heaven."

Christians must reread Genesis 1:28 and the Great Commission (Matthew 28:18-20) and recognize that the Bible *requires us* to be transformers of the culture. We must make a conscious decision to repudiate our old "media mindset" and refuse to see the media as enemy-infested territory that is beyond all hope of redemption. Remember, the "cheap revolution" has provided Christians with an historic window of opportunity to share the gospel, proclaim absolute truth, and phenomenally impact the entire world in ways that simply did not exist even ten years ago. In that way, we can be opportunistic.

Let us covenant together, you and I, to reform the media for Christ. This book is an impassioned plea for you to get on your knees, ask God for wisdom and strength, and then roll up your sleeves and *engage this culture for Christ.* This plan lacks one essential ingredient; without that ingredient the plan cannot succeed. That ingredient is *you.*

Innovation

Christians have long been criticized for producing

sub-par media and, sadly, too often that accusation is accurate. However, times have changed. The *ability* to innovate has always existed for the few who were directly involved in the media. Now, however, because of the new technologies that exist, the *opportunity* is also here for the Christian church as a whole to set the standard for the media by generating good, solid media products and disseminating them to the culture at large.

Dictionary.com defines *innovation*: "to introduce something new; make changes in anything established." Innovation enables us to develop new products and processes creatively. Christian innovation should involve thought, discussion, and prayer. Anyone can be mediocre. It is the innovators in the American culture who reap the largest rewards. Anyone can be good—it takes a unique innovator to be great.

Thomas Edison tried and tried, and after several thousand tries, he was successful in inventing the light bulb. His name is still synonymous with innovation, well over a century later. Bill Gates dropped out of Harvard to run his software business. Today he is the richest man in America. In the 1990s, Matt Drudge, working on a laptop computer from his home, decided to gather stories that the MMD was ignoring and make them available to readers on the Internet. This last time I visited his site, I noted that nearly seventeen million others had visited the Drudge Report during the past 24 hours.

The Innovative Blog

Hugh Hewitt's book, *Blog*, chronicles the rise to prominence of the "blogosphere," a growing network of independently operated web logs. A web log, more commonly known as a "blog," is a personal journal maintained on the Internet by an author or group of authors. Most blogs are updated frequently, and often provide links to other blogs or websites. The blogosphere has created a forum in which tens of thousands of people can have their opinions, facts, and speculations read by thousands of people in a free environment. *That* is innovation.

Hewitt describes in great detail how the blogosphere was directly responsible for the toppling of four men from positions of power and influence: *New York Times* editor Howell Raines, Senate Majority Leader Trent Lott, presidential candidate John Kerry, and CBS news anchor Dan Rather. The Rather story is a powerful example of this phenomenon.

On September 8, 2004, just two months before the American people would go to the polls to choose between George W. Bush and John Kerry, *60 Minutes Wednesday* ran a story which claimed that Bush had performed very poorly during his stint with the Texas Air National Guard, had disobeyed direct orders, and that his commanding officer, Lieutenant Colonel Jerry B. Killian, had been pressured to give Bush a better performance rating than he deserved. Colonel Killian died in 1984, but *60 Minutes* produced memos, purportedly written by Killian, which were offered as evidence.

"The Killian memos," Hewitt explains, "were forgeries. In fact, they were bad forgeries." Within hours of CBS posting the "Killian memos" on their website, stories began to pop up on the blogosphere questioning their authenticity. Bloggers pointed out that the memos appeared to be computer generated. In the early 1970s, when Killian was said to have written the memos, the type fonts in which the memos were printed could only be created using typesetting equipment, which an Air National Guard colonel certainly would *not* have used to write a performance evaluation on a junior officer. Twenty-four hours later, the preponderance of evidence pouring in from the blogosphere had proved that the memos were forgeries. Clearly, CBS had been provided with false documents and, in the rush to break the story, had failed to properly authenticate the memos. Hewitt recounts the results:

> On September 10, during the height of the controversy, bloggers had been dismissed by an ex-CBS big, Jonathan Stein, as just "guys in pajamas." This attempt to sow the impression bloggers were semi-obsessed losers ranting away and venting their frustrations to other losers in a self-contained circle of fanaticism immediately backfired, as the humor-obsessed bloggers embraced the term. Jim Geraghty of KerrySpot … coined the term *Pajamahadeen* and the incredible power of the new medium to define any story was evident. Turning an attack back on the attacker was the defining moment of episode for the blogosphere's future. Only fools will try that gambit in the years ahead, and Mr. Stein's place in the history of journalism is right up there with fellows who served up Ruth's, Aaron's, and Bond's record-setting swings.
>
> The truth was and remains that many bloggers had credentials and résumés far exceeding those of "journalists" who had often spent entire careers in one

organization with little experience outside their own tightly managed and self-reinforcing world. In the middle of Rathergate, the blogger **Beldar**, a very experienced trial and appellate lawyer who had once in fact defended CBS before the Fifth Circuit Court of Appeals, did an extensive post on the credentials of the major bloggers on Sunday, September 12, demonstrating that the MSM really didn't want to follow up on this line of counterattack.[89]

On September 20, Rather publicly admitted, "I no longer have the confidence in these documents that would allow us to continue vouching for them journalistically. I find we have been misled...."[90] CBS fired *60 Minutes* producer Mary Mapes and Dan Rather resigned the following year.

The intriguing aspect to this story is not the professional collapse of a national news anchor, it is the fact that a group of citizens were able to force the media of mass deception to police itself and admit it was wrong. Charles Johnson, of the blog "Little Green Footballs," told the *Washington Post*, "We've got a huge pool of highly motivated people who go out there and use the tools to find stuff. We've got an army of citizen journalists out there."[91] "Rathergate" was the media revolution's shot heard round the world in the press. An army of citizen journalists! This is innovation. As Christians who proclaim that Christ is Lord of all and serve a God who is creative, artistic, and innovative, we, as His image bearers, should be ready to take those characteristics and apply them to the world of media.

Innovative Websites

Entrepreneur Chris Wyatt took an idea and turned it into a phenomenon called GodTube. As of this writing, GodTube is the fastest growing website on the Internet with several million visitors to the site each month.[92] The site allows Christians to upload self-produced or pre-produced material, such as music videos, to one central site. In some cases, videos produced by people in their living rooms are enjoying a larger viewership than network TV shows. Although YouTube arrived on the scene first, Chris Wyatt and GodTube are a great example of innovation in the Christian media realm. They have effectively built a worldwide distribution system that anyone in the world can use to share his or her faith.

Another website under development was the brainchild of Rev. John Sorensen, head of the worldwide relational evangelism equipping ministry, Evangelism Explosion International. EE's site, www.whatsmystory.org, allows Christians to upload their personal testimonies of how they came to Christ and how Jesus has transformed them. Paul commended Timothy for being faithful to make "the good confession in the presence of many witnesses" (1 Timothy 6:12), and Evangelism Explosion is now presenting us all with a unique opportunity to do that very thing. John's prayer is to have one million written and video testimonies uploaded to the site in multiple languages—making it possible for anyone in the world to search and see how Jesus Christ has transformed one million lives.

Innovative Content and Distribution

In my role as President and CEO of Coral Ridge Ministries, I repeatedly preach two things to our staff: content and distribution. These are the essential elements of media. Content is the message and how you craft it. Distribution is how you get that message out to people. We can be innovative with the content we produce or with how we distribute it, but something special happens when we are innovative with both at the same time. This is one of the things I like so much about GodTube. It does just that. It allows users to generate innovative content, and it provides an innovative distribution system.

The changes in Internet, radio, and television provide tremendous potential for Christians to inject innovation into the media today and thereby attract significant attention. We live in the age of the "new media," where innovation is rewarded with a significant number of readers, viewers, and listeners. The risks associated with innovating are very, very small, because the costs involved in innovation are a fraction of what they were even ten years ago.

The influence that Matt Drudge wields in America today serves as an example. He is reaching nearly twenty million people *every day* at an astonishingly low cost per person. So we must ask ourselves the question: How do we become even more innovative in our development of content and our distribution of it? Twenty years ago, you would have had to invest a great deal of money to develop compelling content and then spend even more money to distribute it. Today it's far easier and less expensive.

As discussed earlier, it is now easy to publish your own book, whereas twenty years ago you had no choice but to go through a publishing house. Today there are any number of low-cost services, including Xulon Press and many others, which allow authors to print on demand—whether they wish to reproduce 50 copies or 500,000.

Musicians have also discovered that their distribution

options are expanding. Even some major names are considering abandoning the traditional model of producing CDs and moving to the new model of distributing music solely over the Internet. This model saves an enormous amount of seed money, because the bulk of the costs and expenses related to music are consumed in the actual production and marketing of a specific product. Today, with MP3s, an artist can open a website, put out some smart advertising, and provide a good quality product to a decent number of people.

Truly there is a brand new democratic process in the "new media" that allows Christians an enormous opportunity to develop top-notch content *and* to engage in worldwide distribution. In 2006, Coral Ridge Ministries had some 6.3 million visitors to our website. Thanks to all the work of our radio and television ministry, we now have hundreds of hours of audio and video content on the site that any visitor can access at no charge. We are fulfilling our mission of producing high impact media to proclaim biblical truths that will produce personal and cultural transformation through the inspiration of the Holy Spirit. We are able to reach more people all over the world than we ever have before, and we are doing it in ways that allow our ministry dollars to stretch farther than ever before.

As new media technology and venues continue to establish themselves, and as the old architecture of the media of mass deception continues to collapse, the church has the opportunity to innovate in wonderful ways not available in years past. Just as the light from a match struck in a dark room illuminates the entire space, a little bit of truth can illuminate the hearts and minds of millions of people. Even a relatively small portion of absolute truth can dispel fifty years of dark humanist lies.

Our ability as Christians to innovate—to create content and develop new lines of distribution that reach far beyond what currently exists—is essential to any plan that expects to transform the culture for Christ by providing biblical media.

An Example: Learn to Discern

One of the ways Coral Ridge Ministries is innovating is our "Learn to Discern" viral video campaign. Learn to Discern is a ninety-second video we produce when we spot the media of mass deception using one of its tactics to influence the way people think about a particular issue. We don't attack the messenger and we don't play mean; we simply report the story that was presented as fact in the mass media. Then we ask one question: But is that true? We go from there to present two or three arguments that demonstrate that what the MMD media said was *not* true, allowing the viewer or listener to hear both sides.

Here is an example. There have been a few prominent atheists who have gained some notoriety by making statements based on the popular lie that more people have been killed in the name of God than anything else. Therefore, they claim, all religions are inherently evil. Most Christians instinctively disagree with this conclusion, but they struggle to articulate the reasons why. Coral Ridge Ministries is prepared to arm the body of Christ with some easily-remembered facts that equip us to calmly and intelligently demolish this proposition. We open our segment with a video clip of the atheist asserting that more people have been killed in the name of God than any other reason, and then the host asks: "But is that true?"

The answer is that the argument is demonstrably false. In the twentieth century alone, more than 100 million people were slaughtered in the name of atheism. Atheism—the insistence that there is no God—is the underpinning of the philosophy that drove Joseph Stalin, Adolph Hitler, Mao Zedong, and Pol Pot to slaughter well over 100 million people. If one were to accumulate the death toll of all the people who have died in all the "religious" wars of all of human history, that total would be exponentially dwarfed by the bodies of the 100 million people exterminated in the name of atheistic socialism.

A second argument is this: What do you mean by "in the name of God?" Whose "God" are we talking about? Many non-Christians are quick to lump the god of Islam together with the Judeo-Christian God. It is easy to point out, using both the Bible and the Koran, that these two deities are distinct. Lumping Muslims and Christians and Jews all together and suggesting that all three groups are equally to blame for the nearly 3,000 people who died in the 9/11 terrorist attacks is false.

Our ninety-second clip responding to falsehood and proclaiming truth will rapidly spread all over the Internet using central video sites like GodTube and a number of other viral video message centers. We are enlisting an email army that is committed to sending these videos to as many people as they can. Our message includes a call to action that urges both new viewers and regular "Learn to Discern" users to pass the message on. Within twenty-four hours, perhaps hundreds of thousands of people will watch a ninety-second clip which very politely, neatly, and completely shreds a popular lie. On top of that, we are provided with potential media lies—not by our researchers or staff members—but by you, our viewers. You have the ability to submit video, audio, or print clips that you believe are lies—and we do the rest.

In years past, here is how Coral Ridge Ministries

responded to these atheistic claims. We held a series of production meetings and decided to create a thirty- or sixty-minute television special about *The New Face of Atheism*. We would go into production at significant expense and then add to that the additional cost of buying air time in strategic markets around America. The special would take several weeks and tens of thousands of dollars to produce. The bottom line: the atheists' statement would have lingered in the cultural "air" for so long that by the time our ministry was able to organize a response to the false suggestion, the notion would have been accepted as factually correct by millions. Instead, Coral Ridge Ministries is now able to quickly respond to false claims in the media and disseminate the truth in record time to a large number of people.

The new shape of modern media gives Christians the ability to promptly respond to falsehoods in the MMD, to reach a huge number of people with the truth at very low cost, and to correct distortions before they settle into the minds of millions of Americans. Better still, it provides *you* with an unprecedented opportunity to become a part of the solution—a part of the plan to transform the media for Christ and for biblical truth.

INTELLIGENCE

The skill of disciplined thinking is becoming a lost art in our day, when we tend to have instant everything. We drink instant coffee, play an instant lottery, withdraw instant money at the ATM, and eat instant food from the microwave oven. When we want information about a particular issue, we expect to get instant answers, after a quick visit to Drudge, WorldNetDaily or Fox News. We have become so impatient that we tend to forget that time, rest, research, and analysis cannot be wholly replaced by the instant information we get at the local fast information site.

The process of becoming articulate and intelligent Christians requires investigation and analysis. One of the primary reasons the church in America today is so silent and undiscerning is because it lacks the confidence to speak authoritatively on important issues, whether it be attacks on the deity of Christ, the inerrancy of Scripture, the importance of traditional marriage, or the sanctity of human life. Tragically, we have allowed ourselves to become ignorant. We have been so busy "amusing ourselves to death," we have become so saturated with entertainment, so *me*-focused, that we have forgotten that life is *not* about us; this life is about obeying God and glorifying Him. Part of that process of obeying God and glorifying Him involves becoming a highly literate and articulate people.

Psalm 1 makes clear that we are to meditate on the Scriptures both day and night. It speaks of the sense of being absorbed in God's Word and being absorbed in prayer, so that we might embody Paul's prayer for the Philippian church:

> And this I pray, that your love may abound still more and more in real knowledge and all discernment, so that you may approve the things that are excellent, in order to be sincere and blameless until the day of Christ; having been filled with the fruit of righteousness which comes through Jesus Christ, to the glory and praise of God (Philippians 1: 9-11).

Christianity is not a religion for the ignorant or the thoughtless. We are to be childlike in our dependence on our heavenly Father, but our faith in Jesus Christ compels us to become articulate and intelligent responders to the culture around us. If we are to become a powerful force in the media today and reintroduce Christian values and thinking back into the culture, we must perform the due diligence necessary to grow in knowledge and discernment. Only then will we be intellectually equipped to approve that which is excellent and reprove that which is ungodly.

This is a principle that is drawn directly from Scripture:

> Let the word of Christ richly dwell within you, with all wisdom teaching and admonishing one another... (Colossians 3:16).
>
> Be diligent to present yourself approved to God as a workman who does not need to be ashamed, accurately handling the word of truth (2 Timothy 2:15).
>
> If any of you lacks wisdom, let him ask of God, who gives to all generously and without reproach, and it will be given to him (James 1:5).
>
> Sanctify Christ as Lord in your hearts, always being ready to make a defense to everyone who asks you to give an account for the hope that is in you, yet with gentleness and reverence; and keep a good conscience so that in the thing in which you are slandered, those who revile your good behavior in Christ will be put to shame (1 Peter 3:15-16).

We do not study our Bibles *solely* to become better Christians in our homes and in our churches. We do so that we might also become better citizens of the land with which God has blessed us. Consider just a few of the outstanding Christians who have made a lasting impact on the world, and think about the depth of their intelligence: Blaise Pascal, John Calvin, C.S. Lewis, Chuck Colson, Francis Schaeffer, and D. James Kennedy. I am convinced that God used these men to change the world around them, in part because of their disciplined effort to investigate, search, analyze, think, ponder, and reflect.

You might read this and silently object, "I'm no Calvin or Kennedy." I'm not either. My reply to you is: If we care enough about Christ and America to expose the lies that have been drummed into the consciousness of our culture for the past fifty years, we will make ourselves available with the skills and talents God has given us. Calvin was a sickly, plain man. Dr. Kennedy was a college dropout and dance instructor. Scripture is filled with the unlikeliest of heroes of the faith. If we are to dismantle the lies, we must find our confidence in Christ. We must thoroughly understand the lie itself and have a command of the truth that dispels that lie. That requires intelligence; intelligence requires effort.

"If you continue in My word," Jesus said, "then you are truly disciples of Mine; and you will know the truth, and the truth will make you free" (John 8:32). Perhaps you are passionate about a specific issue. Let's say you have non-believing friends who reject Christianity because they don't believe that Jesus Christ rose from the dead. You remind your friends that Scripture makes the claim that Christ did rise from the dead. Your friend replies, "Well, I don't believe what the Bible says, and the Koran says something different. How am I supposed to know which one is true?" Here is an opportunity for you to respond with tact and intelligence. You have several points you can share to help your friend see the truth.

You might study and learn how to explain that the Bible is a book without parallel in human history. Written over a period of about 1,500 years, it is completely unmatched in its coherence and consistency. You might point to the Bible's astounding record of fulfilled prophecy. You might recount the lives of the disciples, a ragtag bunch that fled in terror when Jesus was arrested, yet after His resurrection boldly proclaimed the gospel, never recanting their testimony, even when faced with agonizing deaths. Your study would also prove that the Bible is the most well-attested book in antiquity. In the face of this evidence, your friend might still reject the Bible on emotional grounds. That is quite possible. Accepting the Scriptures as the Word of God causes us to radically reevaluate our current lifestyle.

Keep in mind that taking ground back from the unbelief enveloping our country will only occur in direct proportion to our ability to lovingly communicate absolute biblical truth. We must also remind ourselves that the Bible is, in and of itself, completely true, irrefutable, and accurate. But that does *not* mean that there aren't other aspects of life that support biblical truth. God created all of life to reflect biblical truth. This is why we at Coral Ridge Ministries use what I call the "Bible+" method of argumentation.

There were many things that our founder, Dr. D. James Kennedy, did extremely well. But something he did particularly well was present the truth about the Scriptures or a cultural issue with multiple arguments and a variety of sources. This is why the MMD didn't particularly like to interview Dr. Kennedy—he was extremely difficult to best in an intellectual debate.

The phrase "Bible+" describes Dr. Kennedy's method

of refuting the arguments his opponents would throw against the Christian worldview. Bible+ means using Scripture *plus* other sources to construct an irrefutable argument. Dr. Kennedy was never afraid to declare that the truth of Scripture was proof enough for any point, but he was never stopped with the scriptural argument either. The wisdom of this approach is being powerfully illustrated in recent days as atheists like Christopher Hitchens and Richard Dawkins claim that truth can only be found in science and reason. Dawkins dismisses the idea of a personal God as "naïve," and asserts that belief in God is "irrational."[93] Unbelievers frequently accuse Christians of being ignorant or incapable of defending their views outside of Scripture. No one ever dared to throw those accusations at Dr. Kennedy. It was important to him to investigate and prepare himself with *several* defenses to be able to give to anyone who asked him for a reason for the hope he had within him.

So how can we use the Bible+ approach to support the truth of the resurrection of Christ? In his book, *Why I Believe*, Dr. Kennedy devoted an entire chapter to the subject. In addition to the scriptural evidence, which is abundant, Dr. Kennedy pointed to:

- Skeptics who set out to disprove the resurrection of Christ and ended up placing their trust in the risen Savior. (One of these was Lew Wallace, who wrote the book *Ben Hur*.)
- The change of the Sabbath day observance from the seventh day of the week to the first day.
- The institution of the Easter celebration.
- Early Christian art and hymnody.

- The formation of the Christian church, the largest institution in the history of the world, is traced by *all* historians (not only church historians) to the city of Jerusalem circa A.D. 30. The message that cemented that early church together in the face of the most violent persecution was that Jesus Christ was risen from the dead.
- The testimony of Trypho, an anti-Christian writer of that era, who acknowledged the fact of the empty tomb.

Dr. Kennedy thoroughly rebutted various theories that have been proposed to explain away Christ's resurrection.[94] He took the time to investigate so that he was prepared to do exactly as Scripture commands us all to do—to look a hostile unbeliever in the eye and gently, patiently, and reverently defend the Christian faith and proclaim a Christian worldview.

Logical arguments offered calmly and intelligently can be used by the Spirit as well as Bible verses. Using the Bible+ method of argument requires us to investigate and arm ourselves with information so that we can gently instruct those who oppose us. The Apostle Paul was thoroughly trained in the Old Testament Scriptures as a young man. Yet we see throughout the New Testament that when he would go to a new city, he employed intelligence, reason, *and* Scripture to support his specific points. He had invested the time to build a vast knowledge of culture, society, history, and law, which he interwove with the Scriptures in order to craft arguments that the Holy Spirit used to pierce the hard hearts

135

of unbelievers.

Christians must master the principles of engaging in good, healthy debate. Whether we are disputing the words of an atheist or a pro-death supporter, we should view the exchange as an opportunity to teach with love and compassion and use intelligence and a sound apologetic presentation.

8

INFORMATION

Innovation and intelligence are vital for engaging in the *media revolution*. These two components are necessary for us to use in developing and sharing arguments informed by a Christian worldview. In the first part of this book we explored the tactics the media of mass deception have used to silence Christians and harm the culture. The media revolution now presents an opportunity for those holding to a Christian worldview to undermine, diminish, and even subvert the effectiveness of those tactics by turning the tables on them. An innovative, intelligent community can use these same tactics to proclaim truth and dispel deception with widely dispersed and well-documented facts. In other words, we can spread truthful information.

A Few Basics

There are a few fundamental principles we should be aware of when we share information through the media:

1. Sharing truth is an act of selflessness, not selfishness.
2. Truth will offend.
3. Act with gentleness and respect.

1. Selflessness, Not Selfishness

Communicating Christian worldview information requires courageous, selfless action. Courageous action must spring from a deep passion that comes from understanding the truth and wanting it spread—not for selfish purposes and not because we desire to be "right," but rather because our hearts ache for the wellbeing of other people. This is often misunderstood today; sometimes it is deliberately misrepresented. The MMD brands us as "intolerant" when we take a position for truth. If our actions are genuinely intended for the greater good of our fellow man, they are not acts of selfishness.

Perhaps the most emotionally combustible issue confronting the culture today is the steady advance of the homosexual agenda. There are two components for the Christian regarding this issue. The first is stopping the advance, using all reasonable means, so that the sanctity of marriage is protected and preserved. This is beneficial for the culture as a whole. The second is helping thousands of homosexuals realize that they are leading a destructive and potentially deadly lifestyle and providing them with loving support.

Many Christians retreat from this topic because they

fear being tagged as "bigoted" and "intolerant." Personally, I am repulsed when I hear of groups that go around carrying signs with hateful slogans like "God hates fags!" This is a terrible misrepresentation of the Christian community and of God Himself. God does indeed hate homosexuality. He hates all sin. But because of God's incomprehensible love, His Son came and died on the cross for your sins and mine. Is the former homosexual any less welcome in the kingdom of God than the man or woman who has committed adultery? We celebrate when we hear stories of alcoholics, cheaters, liars, and violent people who have repented of their past and come to Christ. We should celebrate for a repentant homosexual as well. "Such were some of you," wrote the apostle Paul, "but you were washed, but you were sanctified, but you were justified in the name of the Lord Jesus Christ and in the Spirit of our God" (1 Corinthians 6:11).

Spreading truth about the dire consequences of the homosexual lifestyle is not an act of bigotry or intolerance. It is an act of love that we must embrace. If we can help turn a man or woman away from the intense emotional pain and potential for disease that statistics show is so prevalent among those who engage in the homosexual lifestyle, we are bringing health, joy, beauty and peace into their lives, even through the painful proclamation of the truth. So the truth must be communicated with respect, with professionalism, and with love—but it must be communicated nonetheless.

2. Truth Will Offend

Christians in America today who are seeking to live their lives according to the teachings of Scriptures are required to hold positions that will not endear them to the culture at large. Christians have been (and will continue to be), called all sorts of names, including intolerant and bigoted.

I am no different from anyone else; I would *love* to be liked by everyone. Every emotionally healthy human being would prefer to be liked by his or her fellow man, rather than disliked. But our faith in God compels us to share biblical truth, even when it will offend. For that reason it is a contradiction to call Christians "intolerant and bigoted." Intolerance and bigotry are hallmarks of selfishness and pride, not love. If the following results could occur when we communicate truth, can we still be accused of acting out of selfishness and pride? For by sharing truth in love it is possible that we may:

- Convince someone of the Lordship of Christ, leading that someone to eternal life in heaven
- Rescue someone from the grip of addictive and destructive sin
- Remove violence from a home
- Save the lives of babies and the elderly alike
- Restore a high level of value to the human existence
- Save a marriage
- Promote peace, decency, and human freedom

Using media to proclaim the truth in love, even if it hurts, is an act of obedience, selflessness, and courage. Even when an insulting response is returned against us, we must maintain an attitude of respect, gentleness, intelligence, and compassion.

3. Act with Gentleness and Respect

I once heard a psychologist say, "When someone runs out of things to say, they hit." I have seen plenty of Christians who, confronted with furious *ad hominem* attacks, "hit back" with words. Instead of the enemies of biblical truth being embarrassed by the loving and gentle responses coming from the Christian, the *Christian* is shamed by behaving in a way that fails to display the love and the wisdom of Christ. This is contrary to 1 Peter 3:16-18, which counsels us to use gentleness and respect, even in the midst of heated rebuttals.

We might employ the "feel, felt, found" technique that many salespeople learn for handling objections. When confronted by an opponent who is accusing us of "forcing religion on the rest of America," instead of growing irritated by his hatred and irrationality, we may calmly *and lovingly* reply, "I understand how you **feel**. I've known a lot of folks who **felt** exactly the same way you do, until they **found** out that...." At that point we can supply the antagonist with new information that, God willing, will cause them to see the topic in a new light.

Using Intelligence and Information to Turn the Tables on the MMD

Earlier in this book we looked at the tactics that the media of mass deception have employed to intimidate and silence Christians. Christians can use those very same tactics to turn the tables on the MMD and bring truth back into a dark world. Before we take a look at the last "I," "Infiltration," let's take a look at a few examples of the tactics mentioned earlier in the book which we can use to turn the tables on the media of mass deception. In this way, we can use false information to promote truthful information.

New Names for "The Name Game"

The easiest way for Christians to defeat the "name game" in the media is to use truthful words and phrases. We should refuse to play by their rules any longer. I have explained to you that I do not use the term pro-choice; I use pro-death. Instead of gay, I always say homosexual; instead of speaking of "fundamentalists," we refer to those who hold a Christian worldview. Instead of hate crimes legislation, we should warn of the danger of "thought" crimes legislation. If we are ever to bring truth to light, we must begin to use words accurately and carefully. We must consciously reject any language that promotes the agenda set by the enemies of Christ.

As more and more people begin to use correct terminology in the media and marketplace, the original and incorrect terminologies lose their meaning and impact. If the 80% of Americans who accept that Jesus was resurrected rejected the term "pro-choice" in favor of "pro-death," or "pro-abortion," we could quickly see a shift in the approval of abortion as a common practice. It is that powerful of a technique. It takes time and consistency, but it works.

As you see the MMD introduce new terminology to deceive people, refuse to adopt their nomenclature. Insist on using truthful words and labels that accurately describe. As the democratization of America's media gives you more power and influence, be adamant about speaking the truth in love.

Beating Back "The Blitz"

The media of mass deception has been bringing on "the blitz"—the sheer volume of repeated messaging—for decades. Fortunately, there are a great many alternative sources of media that are beginning to counteract the

MMD blitz, and we can certainly add to these. There is undoubtedly a powerful effect caused by the voluminous amount of material that gushes forth from the other side in the cultural war that we're fighting.

The MMD has long had a great advantage over Christians, due to the sheer mass of humanist material they develop. Nevertheless, the advent of "new media" brings opportunities that did not exist before. Christians can use these media to increase the amount of God-glorifying content they are producing, thus taking ground back from the MMD. Already we are seeing an increase in Christian-based media. More websites and blogs are popping up. Organizations are developing email groups to spread relevant news and commentary. Major movie firms are releasing more movies that appeal to a Christian worldview, and we are seeing a growing assortment of Christian books and music infiltrate major retailers like Wal-Mart, Sam's Club, and other places.

Another example of how CRM is using the Truth Blitz is our *Ten Truths* series, which we launched in 2007. *Ten Truths About Abortion* is complete and, God willing, another project—*Ten Truths About Christians and Politics*—will be completed in the spring of 2008. Another, *Ten Truths About American Christian Heritage*, will debut in the summer of 2008. *Ten Truths* adapts the "Learn to Discern" model by identifying lies that the media of mass deception feeds to the culture and providing clear, concise arguments to rebut those popular myths.

We use a multimedia approach: a brief pocket-size booklet gives readers clear, concise, and well-documented information; a DVD presentation allows viewers to see video clips that flesh out the concepts presented in the booklet; and *Ten Truths* web content allows the individual who wants to dig deep into a particular topic to research supporting audio, video, and print resources.

Coral Ridge Ministries' four main channels of distribution are television, radio, print, and the Internet. When we launch our latest media package in the *Ten Truths* series, we advertise it on television; we interview writers, producers, and key figures on radio; we use Internet channels to market it; and, of course, the core of the product is the print material itself. This strategy allows us to maximize the new media channels in order to gain the maximum exposure for our message. We purchase Google click ads; we link to bloggers' networks to help us spread the word; we produce viral videos that go up on GodTube and other central video sites as well as our own website. We are constantly looking for ways to innovate; watching technology that is expanding at an ever-accelerating rate so that we can take advantage of the latest breakthroughs. Truthful information—spread wisely and cost effectively.

It's a Truth Blitz

Whether you are a member of a large ministry like ours, or you are working alone from home, you still have an opportunity to develop top-quality content—be it music, text, or a viral video. You also have the advantage of using distribution methods that are extremely inexpensive to get your content seen by far more people today than any of us had dreamed of even five years ago. You can become part of the "truth blitz."

One word of caution here: not everything that is created needs to be distributed. Being a musician at heart, I have had the pleasure of writing many songs over the years. Let me be the first to suggest that you can raise a grateful prayer to heaven that most of the songs I've written never made it to any audience's ears. We must never sacrifice quality and professionalism at the altar of quantity. It is important to be *very* discerning about the quality of any material we produce and distribute.

We like to bat around ideas for new and innovative products at Coral Ridge Ministries. But many of the ideas we generate never make it to production. Some of those that do never make it to distribution. It is wise and biblical to enlist the support of many counselors and to ask godly people to review what we produce to make sure that:

- It gives glory to God.
- It is scripturally accurate.
- It meets an internal litmus test for quality before it actually goes out the door.

We have a number of these quality control tests at Coral Ridge Ministries. The first test is whether the theological content aligns with the Scriptures. The second test is whether it aligns with the mission, vision, and values of the ministry. Third, the material must meet high standards for its professional quality in its look, its content, and its production quality. Fourth, everything we produce must have the approval of our executive staff before it is released to the public.

Even if you are working by yourself on your own project, it is crucial to get objective feedback and subject your content to a rigorous review process, whether you are generating a simple blog or writing a song or teaching a children's Bible lesson. As Christians we are to examine ourselves, search the Scriptures daily (Acts 17:11), consider the positions of trusted teachers, and carefully review what we have produced to make sure that it is not only accurate, but that it is fresh, innovative and intelligent. Then it will be of interest to others and will gain their attention.

Besides generating truthful content ourselves, there is a second way in which we can work to defeat "the blitz," and that is to refuse to patronize media sources that promote an anti-God, anti-Christian worldview. Every time we pay to watch an inappropriate movie, or purchase music that encourages us to live for self and not for Christ, or turn on our radio to listen to a vulgar talk show host, or watch television broadcasts that are godless and tasteless, *we are helping perpetuate those messages.*

We have seen that the vast majority of the MMD exists to generate the sale of advertising dollars. Higher ratings mean greater ad revenues; so whenever we buy, rent, watch, or listen to these godless messages, we are actively helping the secular humanist blitz to continue. If Christians in America were to decide to put their dollars where their values are, the dollars involved in producing inappropriate content would dry up and the MMD blitz would cease.

Evening Up the "Odd Men Out"

"Odd man out" seeks to make Christians feel like they are in a tiny, insignificant minority. The solution to defeating this tactic is to use media to connect with other like-minded believers. Talk radio, the blog network, and ministries like Coral Ridge Ministries, Focus on the Family, the Family Research Council, and the Alliance Defense Fund have done a lot of great work to build these connections among Christians in America.

Nevertheless, a majority of Americans continue to remain silent, both at the polls and on cultural issues. One of the ways we can change that trend is to diligently work to connect with them and provide them with information that helps them establish a level of confidence that they, in fact, are not isolated.

I have commented on Rush Limbaugh's enormous contribution to this process, but long before Rush came on the scene, the late Marlin Maddoux was laboring to connect Christians who held to traditional values through the vehicle of talk radio. Pioneers like Limbaugh and Maddoux brought millions of men and women out of the woodwork who thought that the entire country had fallen into an irreversible decline. Talk radio continues to lead the countercharge today, bringing people together, equipping and encouraging the grass roots, and helping to spawn still more celebrities and spokespeople for traditional American values.

Talk radio is just one example how "odd man out" can be defeated. Online communities, blog networks, and centralized information websites provide excellent opportunities to virtually connect with others who hold to the Christian worldview. A great many pastors in America, who frequently feel alone and isolated in their churches, can and should effectively use the media revolution to their advantage to connect with others and broaden their own spheres of influence.

Intelligence and Grace

There can be no doubt that many pastors are silent on cultural issues because of "the silence of the lambs." Christians, both clergy and laity alike, have been bullied into silence because of the perceived unpopularity of taking a moral stance. This tactic is best deflected by heeding the scriptural admonition not to descend to the level of vitriol and sarcasm that so many of our opponents display, but rather to respond with intelligence and grace. "In all things show yourself to be an example of good deeds," the Apostle Paul urged, "with purity in doctrine, dignified, sound in speech which is beyond reproach, so that the opponent will be put to shame, having nothing bad to say about us" (Titus 2:7-8). Elsewhere, Paul instructed young Timothy:

> The Lord's bond-servant must not be quarrelsome, but be kind to all, able to teach, patient when wronged, with gentleness correcting those who are in opposition, if perhaps God may grant them repentance leading to the knowledge of the truth, and they may come to their senses and escape from the snare of the devil, having been held captive by him to do his will (2 Timothy 2:24-26).

Kindness and gentleness are effective tools to employ in every facet of media communication because when we let the truth speak for itself, without injecting inappropriate passions and emotions, we provide an opportunity for those who disagree with us to engage in reasoned discourse. "Come now, and let us reason together," the Lord urged the rebellious people of Israel, and that should be our invitation to those who are in opposition to us, as we gently correct them and graciously lead them to a knowledge of the truth.

If our opponents reject our offer to dialogue together, they eventually shame themselves, because they have descended to a level of shrill argumentation that is not profitable or edifying to anyone. The "silence of the lambs" is best overcome by Christians who represent Christ as He represented Himself—with great intelligence, genuine loving-kindness, and unfailing grace. We are to be strong and courageous, trusting that the Lord our God will be with us wherever we go (Joshua 1:8-9).

In a remarkable exhortation to the church at Corinth, the Apostle Paul exulted in the strength that Christ bestows on every believer, and then urged us to walk boldly in that strength:

> But thanks be to God, who always leads us in triumph in Christ, and manifests through us the sweet aroma of the knowledge of Him in every place. For we are a fragrance of Christ to God among those who are being saved and among those who are perishing; to the one an aroma from death to death, to the other an aroma from life to life. And who is adequate for these things? (2 Corinthians 2:14-16).

We must always remember—the truth is on our side. There is no reason to be silent. The war is already won. We have the obligation and confidence to address cultural issues using the media.

Noah Built the Ark

"Didn't Moses build the ark?" is my way of reminding the church that we have forfeited a rich spiritual heritage of wisdom and knowledge for entertainment and self-satisfaction. We Christians must stop pursuing the pleasures that the culture dangles in front of us and immerse ourselves and our families in the Word of God. We must commit ourselves to education and resolve to eliminate distractions. You have probably heard the saying, "The good is the enemy of the best." There are a great many *good* things we can be doing which will distract us from the *best* thing—which is to "grow in the grace and knowledge of our Lord and Savior Jesus Christ" (2 Peter 3:18) and to raise our children "in the discipline and instruction of the Lord" (Ephesians 6:4).

A special word to fathers: You, to a large extent, will determine the future of this nation by raising a generation of young men and women who do not suffer from the biblical illiteracy that currently afflicts the church. It is ironic that there are more opportunities today for Christians to engage in biblical and theological studies than at any time in history, yet most of our children know a great deal more about celebrities and computers than they do about the living and active Word of God.

We are what we consume. We *must* set the right tone for our children by regulating and monitoring what is consumed by all members of the family. This is a discipline; it is a matter of obedience; and there is no simple way to do this except to pray for God's wisdom and guidance and then just go and do it!

With a commitment to innovation and intelligence, Americans who hold to a Christian worldview have vast opportunities to create and distribute truthful, high-impact information that sets others free.

9

INFILTRATION

Christian media today is not unlike relational evangelism and missionary outreach. We are confronted with a highly secularized, increasingly anti-Christian culture in America and many other Western nations. But the gospel will infiltrate and pierce hard hearts in many different ways. "For the word of God is living and active and sharper than any two-edged sword, and piercing as far as the division of soul and spirit, of both joints and marrow..." (Hebrews 4:12). Like missionaries who go into the deepest, densest jungles of the Amazon, Christians can infiltrate some of the deepest, darkest places of the media world to promote the loving, reasonable gospel of Jesus Christ and the truth of the Scriptures.

The new media provides abundant opportunity to use technology to reach people in places it was never before possible to reach. Whereas Coral Ridge Ministries used to be confined to TV and radio on mostly Christian stations during non-primetime hours, we now no longer have those restrictions. The following provides examples of CRM's strategies to infiltrate the media of mass deception. While we thank God for the three million-plus people who listen to and view our various programs, we have a long way to go. We need your help to infiltrate the culture for Jesus Christ.

We recently started a form of ministry outreach using Internet search engines. Tens of millions of Americans use Internet search engines, such as Google, Yahoo, and MSN every day. They search for news, driving directions, and consumer items. There are approximately six *billion* searches performed each month on the top five search engines,[95] and the advertisers are lining up to present their messages on search engines.

Search engine marketing, as it is called in the business world, is the most powerful form of target marketing that has ever been available to advertisers. Consider this: a company might spend $1 million or more to produce a thirty-second television commercial, and *then* pay more than $2.5 million to run that ad during the Super Bowl.[96] True, tens of millions of viewers are likely to watch that commercial (if they haven't run out to the kitchen or the bathroom), but what percentage of those viewers have an interest in that specific product or service being advertised? The amount of money invested to persuade even one individual to buy the advertised product or service can be very high.

In contrast to the "scattergun" approach of advertising

in newspapers or on television, when individuals visit an Internet search engine and type in the word "bicycle," they are communicating to the search engine that they are potentially in the market for a bicycle. The search engine only returns information about bicycles to these potential consumers. This practice eliminates a tremendous amount of waste from advertising expenses, because only those viewers who are actively seeking a given product or service will view the ads for it. Advertisers like this cost ratio so much that Internet advertising is expected to overtake that of newspaper ads and become the top generator of advertising revenue by the year 2011.[97]

But Americans are searching for a great deal more than consumer products on the Internet. They also seek out doorways to Satan's playground, typing words like "abortion" and "sex" into the search engine windows. Nearly two million people search for the word "abortion" every month.[98] Many of the young women who are confronted with a crisis pregnancy won't tell their friends or their parents or their pastor, but they will go to the Internet to search for information about pregnancy or abortion. The Internet is private and anonymous. The click of a mouse button can immediately expose a woman to hundreds of abortion centers ready to offer abortion as a quick means of "solving" her problem.

Today in several cities in America, Coral Ridge Ministries is using infiltrative technology to give many of these women an opportunity to encounter the truth and to embrace life. We have, at a reasonable cost, purchased the top slots for the major search engines. When someone who lives in one of our target markets types "abortion" or "abortion pill" or "unwanted pregnancy" into the search engine, the very first web link that pops up will take the viewer to a pro-life site that was designed to lovingly present a woman with the truth about the child that is already forming and growing inside her. She will be invited to call a crisis pregnancy center in her area, where she (in most markets) can undergo a free ultrasound test and hear the heartbeat of her unborn child. She also receives loving Christian counsel from the staff of the center.

The Christians who operate these pregnancy centers will tell the expectant mother about options that will allow her to choose life for her baby. The woman will, when the time is right, be presented with the most important option of all—the one that will allow her to choose eternal life for her own soul through hearing the gospel of Jesus Christ. This "search engine ministry" presents us with an opportunity through one click of a mouse to save *two* lives: the life of the unborn child and the eternal life of the mother. We are using media to infiltrate the MMD and to present the truth about life to women at their deepest point of need.

Once again our web department is cooperating with our television ministry to produce the content for this website. We have reached out to several crisis pregnancy centers that are delighted to partner with us in this venture. "We have talked about doing something like this for years," one center director told us, "but we could never afford it." Today, thanks to the grace of God and the generosity of our ministry partners, "something like this" is a reality. Lives and souls are being saved as you are reading this.

A sophisticated keyword traffic estimator tool projects that more than 80 million searches are performed for the key word "pornography" *every month*.[99] Internet porn is a huge industry; one Internet filter provider estimates that sales were $4.9 *billion* in 2006.[100] At this time there are only a handful of Christian ministries attempting to reach out to men and women who are addicted to pornography on the Internet. (I was amazed to learn that Nielsen Net Ratings estimates that nearly one in three visitors to adult websites is a woman.[101]) There is a tremendous opportunity for organizations to use the vehicle of search engines to reach men and women who are often watching their families fall apart and are desperate to change their lives.

Click the Truth

Here is another example of how CRM infiltrates the MMD: news websites post an assortment of articles on a broad variety of subjects. Several of these sites, which have millions of viewers each year, allow vendors to purchase click-ads that are located adjacent to features. Coral Ridge Ministries has implemented a strategy to utilize this new media. When a news site features a story about an issue that concerns us, we have the ability to purchase an ad next to the article on the site. This ad redirects a viewer to content we have developed that shares truthful information. It costs pennies on the dollar compared to purchasing an ad on TV, yet such ads reach a large number of people.

We now have the ability to pinpoint individuals who are investigating issues from a secular perspective and immediately redirect them to an opportunity to consider the Christian worldview perspective on the same issue. Coral Ridge Ministries has been communicating Christian truth to America for more than thirty years, but God has now given us an unparalleled opportunity. Never before could a Christian ministry go toe-to-toe with the MMD and allow Americans to compare the voice of truth with the secular humanist voice—at the same time, in the same venue.

Does it work all the time on all websites? No. Companies can always reject our ads, citing internal policy—and that has happened. What it does provide, however, is the opportunity for families, churches, para-church organizations, and ministries to spend dollars wisely in order to reach more people with the Truth, and to do so in a cost effective way. Broadcast media used to be passive—a TV or radio show would be on at a certain time and we could decide whether to watch it or not. Today media is interactive.

Technology is expanding at an incredible pace. New opportunities to reach people all over the world are presenting themselves almost daily. Think about MP3 players and cell phones. MP3 players are small, handheld devices that allow the user to download and store hours of music or spoken messages. These players are now imbedded in many cell phones. The user has the ability to connect to the Internet and get sports scores, news, and weather, but they can also access sites that preach and teach the gospel through those various mediums. This is another example of how Christians can use technology and new media to reach and infiltrate the culture. Imagine making Christian content available on audio and video enabled cell phones.

I invite anyone who wants to join the media revolution to consider employing the four I's: Innovation, Intelligence, Information, and Infiltration. Proper use of these four principles will result in rapid and effective progress toward bringing the Christian worldview back into a culture that is saturated with media proclaiming a naturalistic and secular worldview.

10

HOW YOU CAN HELP THE REVOLUTION

The media of mass deception is powerful, but its influence has been most pronounced in America during the past 50 years. Its influence is so pervasive that we must concede it is one of the most powerful—if not *the* most powerful—influences on American culture today. However, we've seen how the media elites, which in the past have controlled virtually all of the forms of distribution, are beginning to lose their grip on both the information and the outlets. What I call the democratization of American media is taking place and the power of the media is coming into the hands of the masses.

Finally we have considered a plan for giving Christians the means to use the exciting new media to bring the Christian worldview back into the forefront of our culture. Such a transformation would turn the media of mass deception into the "media of mass revelation." If we can bring back the Christian worldview as the proper foundation for America's media, a culture that values truth, decency, compassion, and selflessness is not far behind.

Earlier I wrote that *you* are the key factor necessary for the media revolution to succeed. There are many ways that you can get personally involved in transforming America's media. Below are a few more of the practical applications of this plan, which Coral Ridge Ministries is using. We would love to have you participate in what we are doing, but we would be just as thrilled to see you innovatively develop your own ways of joining the revolution.

Search Engine Ministry

I have already explained our CRM search engine ministry projects, but consider how you might use search engines to develop a ministry of your own. Just as Coral Ridge Ministries has harnessed the power of search engines to reach women facing crisis pregnancies by providing information that promotes life rather than destroying it, so can you use search engines for ministry. You can do this by conveying biblically-based information to any group of people looking for information about an issue that touches their deepest point of need.

Here are some ideas. Gambling is aggressively pushing itself into many aspects of American life. In 2006, there were 13.5 outlets that sold a lottery ticket in America for every one that sold a Big Mac.® There are now twenty states that allow either commercial gambling casinos, racetrack gambling casinos, or both.[103] The National Council on Problem Gambling estimates that two million American adults a year are gripped by a "pathological gambling" habit, and an additional four to eight million Americans should be considered "problem gamblers." That means they are "experiencing problems due to their gambling behavior."[104]

If God has laid it on your heart to minister to those who suffer from gambling addictions, you could partner with a ministry or a recovery center in your area and purchase the top web return position for keywords related to gambling on three or four search engines. This is not likely to be an expensive project, but it has the potential for great impact. By purchasing these keyword positions and setting up an informational site on gambling addictions, any person who goes online to search for Internet gambling sites using one of these key words will pull up the link to your site, which would provide that person with information on how he or she can be freed from this insidious addiction.

For a remarkably low cost, you have provided that ministry with a badly-needed resource to help steer men and women who are struggling with gambling—whether they realize it or not—to a place where they can begin to recover. Internet gambling is one of the fastest-growing online industries in the world; an estimated eight million Americans gambled online in 2005.[105] With the growing public acceptance of gambling, you can be sure that figure has already mushroomed. Providing a search engine ministry to Internet gamblers would provide an excellent opportunity to infiltrate the culture.

You might have a particular burden for homosexuals who are struggling to get out of that lifestyle. There is a plethora of information on the Internet regarding homosexuality; very little of it, however, is redeeming or hopeful. Once again you might partner with a ministry to homosexuals and help them to design and build a website. By buying keywords in the area served by the ministry, men or women who are surfing the net to engage in homosexual activity can be reached and given the truth about that dangerous and destructive lifestyle.

Keep in mind that most men and women who are overcome by an addiction have no real sense that there is hope or any way out. What is more, many don't even recognize that they *need* a way out from whatever it is that has ensnared them. Part of our "infiltration" tactic is to get the truth into as many hands as possible. The potential applications for search engine ministries are just about infinite. You can target any behavior that is destructive of morals or culture, any addiction, any theological error, or any false religion. Because so many men and women search the Internet for information about virtually any topic, opportunities abound for Christians to use search engines to shine the light of Christian truth into the prevailing darkness.

Here is a practical exercise for you to perform: Invite three or four friends to a Bible study and ask them to brainstorm with you for a half-hour about all the ways you could use a search engine ministry to minister to people in your community. I would be surprised if you didn't come up with at least thirty to forty ideas of how you could employ one of the most inexpensive ways in the world to reach people with Christ's words of eternal life.

Our team and I would love to dialogue with you on this topic. You can send your ideas on search engine ministry to: mediarevolution@coralridge.org.

Self Publishing

You might have a gift for writing. I've known a number of very talented people who write beautifully and have actually sent material out to publishers, only to have it rejected. I have referred to my first book, *Seven Investment Tales*, as an example of how easy it is to write, publish, and distribute your own book in the age of the media revolution. *Tales* was written, edited, published, and distributed inside of six months. It cost me less than $3,000 to print a few thousand copies of the book, and I recovered my costs easily. $3,000 might seem like a large initial investment, but compared to what it costs to publish books through other mainstream avenues, this is a very viable and easy way to get a book published. Talk to other Christians about joining with you in the process. "If one can overpower him who is alone, two can resist him," Solomon observed. "A cord of three strands is not quickly torn apart" (Ecclesiastes 4:12). You will likely find that there are plenty of Christian believers who would love to partner with you in the process of infiltrating the culture with truth.

Not every book needs to be designed to be a bestseller. Perhaps you have a testimony that would reach others that were ensnared as you were. Perhaps you are highly literate on a particular topic and would like to share that. Being an author, regardless of how many books you sell, enables you to gain entry into places where you can speak, teach, or counsel.

Recall that there are two components to media: content and distribution. You may have a magnificent idea for a book, you may possess excellent writing skills, and you may be able to work with editors who will ensure that your book flows well, but the idea of successfully marketing and distributing your book can still seem like a daunting challenge. Let me encourage you. Our ministry is in the publishing business, and distribution is not nearly as challenging now as it was just a few years ago. Coral Ridge Ministries employs many cost-effective Internet techniques to distribute our products. Naturally, we use the major Internet retailers, such as Amazon.com, but in order to generate demand for our products, we utilize a tactic known as "pay-per-click" advertising.

Here is how it works. A man in Texas goes to the Google search engine and types "media influence on culture" in the window. If you are familiar with search engines, you know that any number of results pop up. The majority of these are "organic" results—the search engine has placed these results on your list as the solution to a number of proprietary algorithms (mathematical equations) developed by the search engine companies. These algorithms are very sophisticated and even a little mysterious. Just as only corporate insiders know the precise recipe for KFC chicken or Coca-Cola, only company insiders at Google know precisely why search results come up in the precise order they do. But it really doesn't matter, because today you can "stack the deck" in your favor. We have already seen that search engine ministry is one way to get your web site to pop up in the top three results. A second way to get your particular product or service considered is through the use of pay-per-click advertising.

"Pay-per-click" means exactly what it implies. You only pay the search engine when someone actually clicks on your advertisement. Ten years ago you might pay several thousand dollars to place an advertisement in the sports section of your local newspaper. Let's say the paper's circulation is 100,000. You paid for the *potential* of

100,000 people seeing your ad and acting on it, but in reality, far fewer than 100,000 would actually do so. So you paid a large fee to reach 100,000 people, when in reality, only a tiny fraction of that number actually read your advertisement with interest and intent to purchase your product or service.

Pay-per-click advertising brings your target audience to you. You contract with a search engine company to display your ad only when someone has actually indicated an interest in your product or service. So if you are marketing running shoes, someone who types "automobile" or "iguana" into the search window will never see your ad. But when someone types "athletic wear" or "jogging" or "sneakers," your ad pops up. Immediately you are way ahead of the newspaper ad, because you have succeeded in placing your ad in front of someone who has demonstrated more than a passing interest in what you are offering and you still haven't spent a penny. You aren't charged for placing your ad until the searcher reads your ad copy and clicks the mouse to learn more about your product or service.

This is the ultimate in target marketing. You can publish a book that only costs you a few thousand dollars to produce and then use the Internet to create demand for your product by using the power of search engines to market your book for a fraction of the investment you would have made just a few years ago. There are other tools you can use as well, such as search engine optimization and website marketing, which will allow you to have tremendous success in getting your message out—quite literally—to the world.

If you have had a burden to write a book that will help promote a Christian worldview, but have rejected the idea because you thought you would never get published, that is no longer an obstacle. Let me suggest a five-step process:

- **First**—write your book.
- **Second**—if you aren't personally acquainted with an editor, go online and solicit bids from the many editing services that advertise on the Internet.
- **Third**—when the editing process is complete, use the Internet to solicit bids from vendors who will do the layout and graphic design for your book. There are a great many services that can do that graphic design work for you.
- **Fourth**—investigate the numerous self-publishing companies that will contract with you to print copies of your book.
- **Fifth**—contact a web vendor about helping you market your book. Better yet, do the research yourself. Think about where you would go to meet the most people who would be interested in reading your book. Create strategies for search engine ministry and pay-per-click ads that are keyed to your topic. If the reader clicks on your ad, you have connected with someone who has already indicated that he or she wants the very type of information you are providing. This kind of strategic Internet marketing allows you to pay a fraction of the expense you would pay to take out an ad on radio, television, or in the local newspaper. Remember that in those more traditional

media, you are paying a great deal of money to broadcast to a mass audience, only a fraction of which is actually looking for what you are providing.

There are three caveats to this suggested process. First, pray about your project. "Unless the Lord builds the house, they labor in vain who build it" (Psalm 127:1). You may think that you have penned the next *Purpose Driven Life*, but unless God's hand of blessing is on your work, you are laboring over something less edifying. Ask God to direct your thoughts, to give you wisdom, to shape your words, to glorify Himself in the product, and to bless those who will read your work. Clearly, prayer is the most important component of everything we do.

Second, at every step of the way, prayerfully use your network of Christian brothers and sisters to help you. Again, this activity should begin with prayer. Ask God to lead you to Christian believers who will share your passion for the completion of the project. If finances are an issue, make your need known. Talk about your project to friends and relatives and continue to build your network. This is not because you are trumpeting your own importance as a prospective author, but because you never know who will hear your story and suddenly say, "My husband works as a graphic designer. He has been looking for some work to do from home." Or "My pastor just self-published a book. Let me ask him what print-on-demand company he used." Or "My wife has been editing copy for the radio station for years, and she really has a heart for the subject you're addressing. Let me ask her if she'd be willing to help you." You never know who can help you.

Finally, when working with outside vendors for editing,

graphic design, publishing, or Internet consulting, pray
that God will lead you in the right direction and employ
a good, healthy dose of common sense. Always get at least
three bids for any service you intend to employ. Ask for
references and check them thoroughly. The print-on-
demand field is still in its infancy. Some of these
companies are very good and will help you immeasurably.
Others are not quite as reputable. Investigate several
different vendors for publishing your book. There is a
great deal of information about print-on-demand on the
Internet; take the time to read up on the subject. Ask
potential vendors for references and check them out.
"Trust in God and keep your powder dry," the pioneers
used to say.

I'd like to present one more thought about publishing
a book. If you are a person who wants to have a greater
voice about a particular issue that the Lord has laid upon
your heart, being a published author is an excellent
way to expand your ministry. An individual who has
self-published and marketed a book has clearly
demonstrated the intellectual ability to articulate
thoughts in a coherent fashion *and* the executive capacity
to successfully shepherd a project from start to finish.
Very frequently, these talents are the only keycard you
will need to open doors to a much larger platform from
which to speak.

You will be amazed at how often the title of "author"
will gain you access to people in positions of authority
and influence. If the Lord has put it on your heart to write
a book, I would certainly encourage you to prayerfully
move forward using the methods I've suggested, to step
out in faith and see your work published and distributed
to people all over the world. Again, the entire process
might cost you as little as $2,000, if you are willing to do

the research and make the contacts you need to complete the job.

Start a Blog

I am convinced that the power of the blogosphere is one of the most important aspects of the democratization of the American media. Blogging gives Christians a marvelous opportunity to expose a great deal of the evil and deception that frequently surrounds the issues about which we care so dearly. Whether it is the historical authenticity of Jesus Christ's life, death, and resurrection; the inerrancy of the Bible; the archaeological evidence for the historicity of Scripture; or cultural issues like the sanctity of life and marriage, the blogosphere provides one of the most powerful ways we can influence American culture today.

As Dan Rather and others have learned to their own dismay, the blogosphere is one area where deception doesn't work well at all. In fact, for those who move in the political realm, the blogosphere has become *the* source of information for those who want to bypass what the media of mass deception provides and get a handle on what is true and accurate. To step into the blogosphere is to stand before a rigorous jury of peers who will meticulously scrutinize what is said by everyone—the MMD *and* fellow bloggers—to make sure that the information is actually valid and valuable.

With millions of people turning to blogs for information every day, it is critically important that the church step into this arena. Currently the vast majority of effort in the blogosphere is directed to the sphere of government and politics. Both the conservative and liberal sides of the political debate have made great use of the blogosphere to effectively promote their specific agendas.

167

If Christians will carry out the due diligence necessary to build a reputation for intelligent discourse and accurate teaching, we will enjoy the same success as the bloggers who have labored to expose the political lies that have become so prevalent in the culture.

Can you imagine what would happen if Christian worldview bloggers banded together and began to transmit accurate, timely information—not about political issues, but about the spiritual and moral issues of the day? Dr. Kennedy once talked about forming a grassroots army of Christians who were mobilized to bring salt and light to specific cultural issues which were pressing upon their communities. That dream can now be realized through the power of the blogosphere.

Here are three suggestions for how you can utilize the blogosphere to make an enormous impact on our culture for Christ. First, at the very least, every Christian should become educated about what is happening in the blogosphere. Consider reading Hugh Hewitt's book, *Blog*, to gain a better understanding of the power of web logs. The blogosphere is rapidly becoming *the* best way to get news, information, and perspective. Being well-informed is extremely important—even if, at this point, you do not feel led to contribute to the discussion. Disciplining yourself to become an articulate, well-informed, well-rounded Christian is vital to reforming our culture today. I cannot overstate that fact.

Second, consider starting your own blog. That might seem like a preposterous idea, especially if you still have only a vague idea of what a blog is. A blog is simply a diary or a statement of information and/or opinion given by one person. You can go to www.coralridge.org and click on our blog section. You will find blogs there written by a number of our CRM staff members.

Your first inclination might be to dismiss this suggestion by saying to yourself, "I'm nobody of any great importance. Why would I start a blog?" That's just it! We are talking about the democratization of the American media. This is a time when ordinary people like you and me have the unprecedented opportunity to make our voices heard in an arena that is not regulated by an elite group of individuals intentionally trying to squelch the Christian worldview. This is the *best* time to start blogging, simply because you now have a voice, along with everyone else. While it is true that web blogs maintained by people of repute often enjoy significant readership, if only ten or fifty or one hundred people read your blog on a daily basis, that is hardly an insignificant number.

Keep in mind that the blogosphere ultimately represents incredible opportunities for networking information. You might maintain a blog that is read by only twenty people; however, one of your readers maintains a blog read by two hundred people, and one of *those* readers has a blog that is visited by two thousand people. Clearly you can see the pyramid effect where you, residing at the apex of the informational pyramid, can begin to influence a huge number of people at the base, even though only a relative handful of them personally read your work. Hugh Hewitt calls it "the swarm."

The blogosphere is all about using other bloggers' information to connect ideas and opinions and views— to hone and refine and sharpen them. It is completely conceivable that a coordinated group of bloggers with only a few hundred regular readers can inject themselves into this massive network and begin to exert significant influence on the culture.

I would issue this challenge: Every time a local

newspaper or a national newscast employs tactics like "the name game" or "say what?" and issues the same old MMD lies about the "separation of church and state" or "a woman's right to choose," that should spark an immediate reaction from a coordinated Christian worldview blogosphere. Whatever false statements or half-truths are issued by the MMD and represented as facts should be promptly and thoroughly dismantled using Scripture, science, history, logic, philosophy, and medicine—using Dr. Kennedy's "Bible+" strategy. This would naturally lead to appropriate action: phone calls to the paper, letters to the editors, emails to congressmen, etc.

Third, we are working to create just such a network at Coral Ridge Ministries called the Learn to Discern Bloggers Network. As soon as we spot a news item that promotes a particular MMD lie, we will respond with accurate information provided by our research staff, coupled with video clips produced by our television department. Consider this as an invitation to join the network! We can disseminate information to millions of people if you help us. See www.coralridge.org for more information about the Learn to Discern Blogger's Network.

If you resonate with an orthodox Christian worldview, and if you are concerned about the current direction of our American culture and the duplicity of the American media, then please take the initiative to start a blog on Townhall.com or one of the many free blog sites. Then you can start using innovative strategies to attract people to your site. The networking power of the blogosphere has already proven to be highly effective in the political arena. There is absolutely no reason why that power can't generate the same kind of impact in the religious, educational, social, cultural, and moral spheres as well.

In case you aren't aware of this, the followers of Islam are already quite busy on the Internet, in general, and in the blogosphere, in particular, promoting their worldview and networking with like-minded people. Do we Christians not have an even greater obligation to fully engage in the media revolution in order to glorify Jesus Christ our Lord and preserve the unique quality of life and religious freedom that Americans enjoy?

If you are already blogging I would urge you to follow the biblical mandates discussed earlier. Christians who are broadcasting hateful, hurtful speech or who promote ideas that aren't supported by Scripture—who are blogging emotional, irrational, uninformed, unintelligent statements—do more harm than good. Nathan's rebuke to David would apply to angry bloggers equally well: "By this deed you have given occasion to the enemies of the Lord to blaspheme" (2 Samuel 12:14).

If you do not consider yourself to be sufficiently saturated with Scripture and possessing practical knowledge about the issues, I would encourage you to sit at someone else's feet and be mentored until such time as you do become enough of an authority on a subject to enter the blogosphere. Or you might consider forming a partnership with a more knowledgeable believer who is not particularly gifted as a writer; in other words, you write and edit the content for someone who is gifted with real knowledge and all discernment.

"Excellence in all things, and all things to God's glory," D. James Kennedy always said. It is important that we develop information in a manner that is consistent with our specific skills and talents—and that we do it in excellence to the glory of God. If you are in agreement with many of history's great Christian thinkers and have a deep heart for the Word of God and understand its application, may I encourage you to tackle those issues in your blog? Coral Ridge Ministries has traditionally focused on six key issues in our media and our programming. While we by no means have limited ourselves to these six topics, we do believe they provide a necessary foundation for our ability to carry out the cultural mandate within our culture and society. These six topics include:

- A biblical view of creation.
- The right to life of the unborn.
- The fight against pornography.
- America's Christian heritage.
- The sanctity of marriage and the traditional family.
- Religious liberty.

If you resonate with any of the issues I have listed here, I would strongly encourage you to join our bloggers network. We are living in an era unlike anything seen before in history. Hugh Hewitt compares our day to the fifteenth century, when the Gutenberg Bible was printed on the first printing press. Shortly thereafter, there was a massive, culture-altering revolution because of the new media of the day—print. According to Hewitt, such opportunity exists once again. Yet this time we now have the ability to transmit accurate information with the click of a mouse or a TV remote. You and I now hold "the power of the pen." We have the power to change our culture by disseminating true, meaningful, life-changing information in ways that perhaps only a handful of visionaries imagined just ten years ago.

Viral Emails

You can reach thousands upon thousands of people by starting what we call "viral emails." The word "viral," which suggests a "virus," may not be the most positive choice of adjectives for a message that rapidly spreads to a large number of people. It is a positive development, however, that you and I can forward good and helpful information to as many people as are in our address book. Viral emails are the fastest and most cost effective way to reach tens of thousands of people with important information and a call to action.

In November 2007, New Jersey voters rapidly mobilized to forestall a threat to traditional marriage. When a state senator introduced a bill to legalize "same sex marriage," groups like the New Jersey Family Policy Council sprang into action, sending out thousands of emails to constituents who forwarded the message on to friends and neighbors, thus generating an avalanche of phone calls to New Jersey's legislative leaders. "It's jamming our phone lines and we can't do our work here," the president of the New Jersey Senate grumbled to reporters. "There's no intention to do the bill," he added. "It's not going to be posted."

The MMD printed "name game" quotes from activists complaining about "right wing, anti-gay campaigns." But the results of the rapid response by concerned citizens were unmistakable: "We nipped something in the bud," the president of the New Jersey Family Policy Council concluded with obvious relief and satisfaction.[106] This is a perfect example of the power of viral emails.

How can you prepare your community to influence the culture in the same way? Begin today to enlist an army of emailers who are committed to addressing the cultural issues of our day. As I've noted, we have entitled our network "Learn to Discern." You might select a different name for your community's mobilization network. The point of the exercise is to create a virtual network of local people who care enough about their community that they are willing to invest just a few minutes each week to protect their quality of life and religious freedoms from the forces of secular humanism and those religions that promote violence and destruction.

Your church is the place to start recruiting for such a group. Form a small study group in your neighborhood consisting of men and women who are concerned about a key issue. Your group might meet once a month. When you do, record the email addresses of all who attend the meetings. Together you can take the initiative to gather information about the work of those groups and legislators who are working to promote godlessness and immorality in your community. Agree to only send emails through this network that conform to its stated purpose. Sending junk email or jokes over the network will result in lost readership.

Make it a practice to *politely* keep your government officials informed of your opinions. The more members who join your network, the easier it will become to influence school board officials and state and local legislators. We still live in a constitutional republic. Our elected representatives—particularly at the local and state levels—are sensitive to the feedback they get from their constituents.

In a time when a great many Americans appear to have become too apathetic to utilize our constitutional right to petition the government for a redress of grievances (which simply means that many of us are too lazy or too "busy" to keep informed and contact our elected representatives), your voice—raised in polite, articulate, informed persuasion—carries great influence. One of the easiest, fastest, and least expensive ways to exert that influence is online. You can connect with likeminded people in your area at many online communities and see if they are impassioned about the same issues that you are.

Viral email is one of the most powerful tools available to us through the new media. It is fast; it is inexpensive; and it is effective. Coral Ridge Ministries frequently employs this form of communication, along with other national organizations like the Family Research Council, Alliance Defense Fund, Focus on the Family Action, and others. But on the local level, which is where you personally have the greatest ability to influence outcomes, there is precious little organized community activity and networking occurring on specific spiritual and cultural issues. I encourage you to pray about how the Lord would lead you to make your voice heard in terms of the issues that are most important to you.

Viral Video

If you are reading this book and don't yet have a high-speed Internet connection, let me strongly suggest that you to set this book down *right now* and begin to investigate how to get it. What was once a luxury is now extremely affordable, thanks to the fierce competition between DSL (Digital Subscriber Line), cable, and satellite providers of high-speed Internet service. The reason I urge you to invest in a connection is because viral video is rapidly becoming one of the most popular and most effective ways that information is being communicated throughout our nation.

The spectacular emergence of GodTube as the fastest

growing Internet site in the world shows that millions have a deep desire to see Christian content spread over the Internet. It is now entirely possible that your video— or a video of your choosing—will be seen by more people than a network television show. Compelling content can be spread using the same technology that drives viral email. Viral video is spread via links embedded in email. If you are a person who is concerned about an MMD lie, get a webcam and record yourself. "A picture is worth a thousand words," and a gripping 90-second video can often generate a greater response than the most brilliantly written text. Send your video embedded in an email to the citizens' network you have assembled and encourage them to send it to others. When CRM created a video for the web that contained a review of the movie, *The Golden Compass*, which was written by proclaimed atheist Phillip Pullman with the intent of teaching kids about atheism, it received thousands of views after it was emailed to our email lists and put on various websites.

Increasingly you will see many major market television and radio shows, plus major Internet sites, utilizing videos created by users to enhance their programming. Once again, if the church can unify itself on these issues, we have an unprecedented opportunity for using this wonderful, democratized form of mass communication to inform, to express views and concerns, and to evangelize—not only in America, but all over the world. I have a vision for thousands of local communities using both viral email and video to act as powerhouses of influence, compassion, and ministry in their area.

These communities of concern *can* become a reality. The technology exists and the costs are minimal. Sometimes I think that the Christian church in America is like a sleeping giant that needs only a nudge and a helping hand to move it out of its lethargy and to get it started down the path to renewed righteousness. As you have read this book, you have been following my thinking about the opportunities the media revolution presents to the church, and we have almost come to the conclusion. I want to exhort you to be one of those pioneer men or women who will give the church that nudge. I challenge you to begin utilizing these inexpensive technologies to communicate, to connect, and to go and make disciples of all the nations, teaching them to observe all that Christ has commanded us (Matthew 28:19-20).

Unrevise the Revisions—Virtually

In 2006 "You" were awarded the *Person of the Year* award by *Time* magazine. This award drew major media attention to the advancing success of user-contributed, online collaboration projects. Broadly deemed "Web 2.0," these online user communities facilitate creativity, collaboration, and sharing between users via the Internet. Examples of successful Web 2.0 web sites are Wikipedia.com, MySpace.com, and YouTube.com. These sites attract millions of contributors and readers each year. Opportunity abounds to share truth through these virtual collaborations.

Wikipedia (http://en.wikipedia.org/wiki/Main_Page) is essentially an open-source encyclopedia. Anyone with an Internet connection can edit any article about any subject in the world. (As of November 2007, Wikipedia had approximately 9.1 million articles in 253 languages comprising a combined total of over 1.41 billion words for all Wikipedias.) The entire web site is completely self-sustaining and is policed only by its users. Essentially, users are redefining the meanings of our understanding of the world around us and whoever is the most persistent, the most intelligent, and the most believable will win out.

Can you imagine what impact would occur if a collection of committed, biblically literate Christians, armed with irrefutable facts, flooded Wikipedia with a Christian worldview perspective? Keep in mind that more often than not, when you search for any topic in a search engine, the first organic (non-sponsored) result is from Wikipedia. The potential influence is staggering.

For example, if you go to Google.com and searched the term "marriage" the very first result that you get in the organic search results is from Wikipedia. It reads:

> Marriage or wedlock is an interpersonal relationship with governmental, social, or religious recognition, usually intimate and sexual. Created as a contract, or through civil process. Civil marriage is the legal concept of marriage.
>
> The most common form of marriage unites a man and a woman as husband and wife. Other forms of marriage also exist; for example, polygamy, in which a person takes more than one spouse (marriage partner), is common in many societies. In some jurisdictions marriage has been expanded to include same-sex marriage.
>
> The reasons people marry vary, but usually include one or more of the following: legal, social and economic stability; the formation of a family unit; procreation and the education and nurturing of children; legitimizing sexual relations; public declaration of love; or to

obtain citizenship.

A marriage is often declared by a wedding ceremony, which may be performed by a religious officiator, through a similar government-sanctioned secular officiator, or (in weddings that have no church or state affiliation) by a trusted friend of the wedding participants. The act of marriage usually creates obligations between the individuals involved, and in many societies, their extended families.

Notice how this definition of marriage differs from the biblical definition of marriage. Can you imagine how the world's understanding of the meaning of the word "marriage" would change if an organized band of Christians committed to policing this and other definitions and provided a biblical truth? Wikipedia is just one of the sources of information attracting millions of searchers each year. In an open source environment like this, Christians can gain a tremendous foothold in providing truth in a secular environment. New media means new opportunity for ministry.

Become a Bible Master Through Technology

Warning: I'm about to do a shameless promotion.

Another way we can engage in the media revolution is to use tools that help us grow in our knowledge of the Bible, and Coral Ridge Ministries is developing computer software that will radically transform your understanding of the Bible and how you study it. CRM has teamed up with Logos Bible Software in Bellingham, Washington, to create a unique tool. Logos has designed what I believe is the premier Bible study software in the world.

Let's say you want to read Psalm 23 and gain a deeper understanding of the passage. The Logos software allows you to compare several different English versions of the Bible along with the original Hebrew text, as well as review the texts of several different commentaries and Bible dictionaries, and then create your own study notes within the software package. You can also see what great hymns of the Christian faith were derived from Psalm 23. I own this software, as do several members of our staff. Without exception, everyone agrees that Logos has provided an incredibly powerful and enriching tool for studying the Bible unlike anything we have seen before. Again, the media revolution is providing us with the technology to help us become more biblically literate Christians in a way that just was not available a few short years ago.

In teaming up with Logos, CRM has taken a step towards a new generation of Bible software. Several years ago, Dr. Kennedy recognized that knowledge of the basic doctrines of our Christian faith is sadly lacking in American churches and he wrote a tremendous book, *Truths That Transform*. The book explains the foundational doctrines of the Christian faith in clear language, which can be easily understood by a high school student. *Truths That Transform* proved to be so popular that it was expanded in 1996 and is now in its fourth printing. Logos Software has embedded Dr. Kennedy's book, along with an extensive study guide and an accompanying audio sermon series, into their Bible study software.

Using this software you can read the book, click a link to hear Dr. Kennedy's original audio sermons (no Internet connection is required), and you can work through a rich, challenging study guide—all without exiting the software program. Whenever Dr. Kennedy references a particular verse of Scripture, you have immediate access to the verse, its various translations, and its original language. The program also gives you instant access to some of the great Reformed thinkers whom Dr. Kennedy references in *Truths That Transform*, such as Charles Hodge. If you would like to listen to Dr. Kennedy discussing the specific doctrine in question, you have the ability to do that—in the time it takes to click the mouse. Using the study guide material, you can study the book in depth, saving your results as you go and instantly checking your answers to the questions against Dr. Kennedy's text and the sample answers provided by our editors.

To the best of my knowledge, no program has ever provided the ability to incorporate the leading-edge technology of Bible study software like Logos with the foundational doctrinal teaching of one of the twentieth century's greatest pastors and teachers. I encourage you to check out a short seven-minute infomercial on this groundbreaking Bible study opportunity at www.coralridge.org/ttt-logos-tour.asp. Also, keep checking our website. You are going to see many more innovative applications of online services, software technology, and curriculum development, as Coral Ridge Ministries continues to develop tools to help the body of Christ pull back the curtain from cultural lies and equip those who care about absolute truth and its application to the culture.

Frankly, as excited as I have been about completing this book and putting it into your hands, I fully recognize that these pages have only scratched the surface of the media revolution that is taking place. There are hundreds, if not thousands, of innovative ideas for how you can utilize the new media to infiltrate the culture and become a part of the movement to defeat, once and for all, the media of mass deception.

If this book has inspired you to spend some time thinking, praying, and meeting with those in your community who are concerned about the future of this nation, then it has rightly served its purpose. And if Coral Ridge Ministries can be of any assistance to you, please contact us. As we continue our battle against the media of mass deception and the cultural lies which have had such a debilitating influence on the American culture, we need for you to join us and share your strategies and successes with us. In this way we can return to being a country that honors its Christian roots, that values human life, that upholds traditional marriage, and that celebrates biblical truth in the mainstream culture.

The American culture has been standing at a crossroads for some time now. I believe we will make an irreversible turn—one way or the other—in this next decade. What we do today will inevitably determine what sort of nation our children will live in. One of the very best ways we can use the new media to bring the Christian worldview back to our culture is by training up our children in the way they should go—not only by showing them how to *use* media, but by teaching them how to *discern* what it is that they're seeing and hearing in the media. Ted Baehr and Pat Boone released an outstanding book, *The Culture-Wise Family*, which addresses this topic in great detail.

You and I were raised in a culture that was, at the very least, tolerant of a Christian worldview. Americans over the age of 50 clearly recall a nation that accepted Christianity as a glorious truth central to our lives. Our children are growing up in a vastly different culture that almost totally rejects the Christian worldview. If the

America of 50 years ago is not to become a land that exists only on the pages of history books, we must immerse ourselves in the ideas and strategies outlined in this book and in the books that I have referenced—and then put them into practice. We must constantly remind our children, our friends, and our elected officials that we no longer live in an informational age dominated by a small, secular media, but we live in an exciting new democratized society, where truth can reign—and *will* reign if we will only bend our shoulders to the task, beseeching God to direct and bless our efforts.

I am convinced that you and I are blessed to live on the eve of a new epoch. Like Gutenberg with his printing press, and the courageous Protestant Reformers who followed on his heels, may we be remembered as men and women who likewise changed the course of history. We have the opportunity to participate in nothing less than the transformation of American culture. The *media revolution* is underway; let us pray for God's direction and join it!

A FINAL WORD

The Media Revolution is about absolute truth. Absolute truth does exist and is the most liberating force in the world today—for those who accept it. You may not believe that absolute truth exists. You may believe that truth is what we make it, what we discover through time, experience, or private revelation.

There was a man in the Roman Empire who, in a quiet moment and faced with a difficult legal decision, asked a poignant question of the defendant: "What is truth?" He waited for no reply. The irony of Pontius Pilate's question was that he was asking the One who is Truth—Jesus the Christ.

There is absolute truth. There is a God in heaven who is holy, just, loving, and sovereign. He is without sin or blemish. He is just. His ways are higher than ours. He is loving, wishing to have a deep, abiding relationship with His creation—mankind. And He is sovereign, fully in charge of every person, every city, every nation, and every government, at all times.

Each and every one of us is a sinner—that is, we disobey God's laws. Think about how many times a month, a week, or even a day that we sin. We think ill of someone. We act out of selfishness. We talk behind someone's back. In every single day of every single year, each and every one of us sins. And those sins add up.

This presents a problem for us. Since God is a holy God, He hates sin. And the Bible says that no one is righteous in His eyes–that our good deeds are like filthy rags. There is absolutely nothing we can do to work, pay, or cajole our way to God.

And so in God's grace and mercy, He sent His one and only Son to earth. This man, Jesus, was God in human flesh. He lived the only sinless life. He was executed, but a few days later broke the curse of death and came back to life. When He was killed, He became a divine substitute for us—taking our sins and bearing the punishment for sin that we justly deserve. Now he offers forgiveness and eternal life in Heaven. He made a way for us to experience God's free and full forgiveness for sin and to have a relationship with the God of the universe.

There is nothing we can do to earn His forgiveness and a place in heaven. It is free. Jesus has bought and paid for our relationship with God in this life and eternal life with Him in the next.

Someone once told me that he wouldn't serve a God like that—One who only provided one way for us to get to heaven. I told him, "The mystery isn't that there is only one way to God, the mystery is that God provided a way at all!"

Friend, we deserve death. But because God is merciful and loving, He has provided His very own Son to restore us to a relationship with Him. All you have to do is accept God's free gift of life through Jesus Christ, His Son.

If you have not already told Jesus that you accept His free gift of salvation from your sins, I pray you do that today. You can pray to God in many ways, but here is a suggestion, if you want peace in this life and heaven in the next:

> Jesus, I am indeed a sinner. I am not worthy of God, heaven, or His grace. But because You came to this earth, died, and

rose from the dead, I now know I can have eternal life. Jesus, forgive me of my sins. I accept you as both Savior and Lord. Come into my heart and save me, Jesus. Thank you.

If you have prayed this prayer for the first time today, welcome to the Family of God. You have become a part of the Real Revolution—the revolution that occurs when a creation of God becomes a child of God.

For more information on what a life with Jesus Christ is about, please visit us at www.coralridge.org.

ENDNOTES

1   All definitions from *Merriam-Webster's Collegiate Dictionary, Eleventh Edition*
    (Springfield, Mass.: Merriam-Webster Incorporated, 2006) 1344, 717, 770.
2   Random House, Inc., *"Letter to a Christian Nation,* Author Interview,"
    http://www.randomhouse.com/catalog/display.pperl?isbn=9780307265777&view
    =auqa (Viewed 12/17/07)
3   Suzanne Bowdey, "Violence and Promiscuity Set the Stage for Television's
    Moral Collapse," Family Research Council: *Insight,* Issue 248,
    http://www.frc.org/get.cfm?i=IS02E4#edn5 (Viewed 12/17/07)
4   Ibid.
5   Parents Television Council, Facts and TV Statistics, "'It's Just Harmless
    Entertainment' Oh really?" Study Conducted by RAND and published in the
    September 2004 issue of *Pediatrics,* http://www.parentstv.org/PTC/facts/
    mediafacts.asp (Viewed 12/17/07)
6   Parents Television Council, "'It's Just Harmless Entertainment'" Study conducted by
    Huston and Wright, University of Kansas, "Television and Socialization of Young
    Children." (Viewed 12/17/07)
7   Michael Weisskopf, "Energized by Pulpit or Passion, the Public is Calling:
    'Gospel Grapevine' Displays Strength in Controversy Over Military Gay Ban,"
    The Washington Post, 2/1/93, A1. Viewed on www.dick staub.com,
    http://www.souljourners.org/links_view.php?record_id=3321 (viewed 12/17/07)
8   Katharine Q. Seelye, "Circulation Plunges at Major Newspapers," *The New York
    Times,* October 30, 2006, http://www.nytimes.com/2006/10/30/business/media/
    31papercnd.html (Viewed 12/17/07)
9   See, for example, the *Project for Excellence in Journalism,* "The State of the News
    Media, 2007: An Annual Report on American Journalism," http://www.stateof
    thenewsmedia.org/2007/narrative_networktv_audience.asp?cat=2&media=5
    (Viewed 12/17/07)
10 Results summarized in *American Life League,* Chapter 124: "The Source and
    Nature of the Media's Biases,"
    http://www.ewtn.com/library/PROLENC/ENCYC124.HTM (Viewed 12/17/07)
11 Ibid.
12 Linda Saad, "Tolerance for Gay Rights at High-Water Mark," The Gallup
    Organization, May 29, 2007, http://www.gallup.com/poll/27694/Tolerance-Gay-
    Rights-HighWater-Mark.aspx (Viewed 12/17/07)
13 ABC News, "New Details Emerge in Matthew Shepard Murder," November 26,
    2004, http://abcnews.go.com/2020/Story?id=277685&page=1 (Viewed 12/17/07)
14 Ibid
15 The Barna Group, "A New Generation Expresses its Skepticism and Frustration
    with Christianity," September 24, 2007, http://www.barna.org/FlexPage.aspx?Page=
    BarnaUpdate&BarnaUpdateID=280 (Viewed 12/17/07)
16 A. Larry Ross and Whitney Kelley, "Seeking the Truth that will Set us Free," reprinted
    by Westminster Theological Seminary, http://www.thetruthaboutdavinci.com/about/

(Viewed 12/17/07)

17   Zogby International, "Support for Abortion in Sharp Decline," January 23, 2006,
      http://www.zogby.com/news/ReadNews2.dbm?ID=1060 (Viewed 12/17/07)

18   Chris McComb, "Teens Lean Conservative on Abortion," The Gallup Organization,
      November 18, 2003, http://www.gallup.com/poll/9715/Teens-Lean-Conservative-
      Abortion.aspx (Viewed 12/17/07)

19   Joseph Farah, *Stop the Presses!* (Los Angeles, Calif.: *World Ahead Media*, 2007) 140.

20   Quoted in *American Life League*, "Chapter 124"

21   The Project for Excellence in Journalism, "The State of the News Media, 2007,"
      http://www.stateofthenewsmedia.org/2007/narrative_networktv_audience.asp?
      cat=2&media=5 (Viewed 12/17/07)

22   William J. Bennett, *The Index of Leading Cultural Indicators* (New York:
      Broadway Books, 1999).

23   David Kupelian, "How the Marketing of Evil Really Works," *WorldNetDaily*,
      December 14, 2005,http://www.wnd.com/news/article.asp?ARTICLE_ID=47885
      (Viewed 12/17/07)

24   Quoted in David Kupelian, *The Marketing of Evil* (Nashville, Tenn.: WND Books,
      2005), 190.

25   David Kupelian, *The Marketing of Evil* (Nashville, Tenn.: WND Books, 2005).

26   Josh McDowell with Bob Hostetler, "Truth and Tolerance," *The Plain Truth Online*,
      September/October 2002, (emphasis in original) http://www.ptm.org/02PT/
      SepOct/truthTolerance.htm (Viewed 12/17/07)

27   Ibid.

28   United States Department of Labor, News, Bureau of Labor Statistics, "Table 8.
      Time spent in primary activities (1) for the civilian population 18 years and over
      by employment status, presence and age of youngest household child, and sex, 2006
      annual averages," http://www.bls.gov/news.release/atus.t08.htm (Viewed 12/17/07)

29   Dale and Karen Mason, *How to Get the Best Out of TV*, (Nashville: Broadman and
      Holman, 1996). Cited in Suzanne Bowdey, "Violence and Promiscuity."

30   See, for example, "The Cooling World," *Newsweek*, April 28, 1975. The article
      concludes, "The longer the planners delay, the more difficult will they find it to
      cope with climatic change once the results become grim reality." Sound familiar?

31   Marcus Baram, "An Inconvenient Verdict for Al Gore," ABC News, October 12,
      2007, http://www.abcnews.go.com/US/story?id=3719791&page=1
      (Viewed 12/17/07)

32   William J. Broad, "From a Rapt Audience, a Call to Cool the Hype," *The New York
      Times*, March 13, 2007, http://www.nytimes.com/2007/03/13/science/13gore.html
      (Viewed 12/18/07)

33   Brian Fitzpatrick, "Another Holiday, Another Plug for Atheism," *Culture Links* 1,
      No. 13 (November 27, 2007).

34   Library of Congress, "Jefferson's Letter to the Danbury Baptists,"
      http://www.loc.gov/loc/lcib/9806/danpre.html (Viewed 12/18/07)

35   Library of Congress, "Religion and the Federal Government, Part One. The State
      Becomes the Church: Jefferson and Madison," http://www.loc.gov/exhibits/religion/
      rel06-2.html (Viewed 12/18/07)

36   Ibid.

37   *Wallace v. Jaffree*, 472 U.S. 38, 105 S. Ct. 2479 (1985), Nos. 83-812, 83-929.

38   CNN.com, "Transcripts, CNN Larry King Live, Interview With Dr. James Dobson,
      aired November 22, 2006," http://transcripts.cnn.com/TRANSCRIPTS/0611/22/
      lkl.01.html (Viewed 12/18/07)

39   Kupelian, "How 'Marketing of Evil' Really Works," http://worldnetdaily.com/news/
      article.asp?ARTICLE_ID=47885 (Viewed 1/4/08)

40   D. James Kennedy, foreword to *The Rewriting of America's History*, by Catherine Millard (Camp Hill, Pa.: Horizon House Publishers, 1991) ii.

41   Catherine Millard, *The Rewriting of America's History* (Camp Hill, Pa: Horizon House Publishers, 1991) 37.

42   Ben Shapiro, "Coddling Pedophiles," *HumanEvents.com*, August 8, 2007, http://www.humanevents.com/article.php?id=21864 (Viewed 12/18/07)

43   Interview with Bernard Goldberg for *The Coral Ridge Hour*, March 11, 2004, Tape R880.

44   L. Brent Bozell III, *Weapons of Mass Distortion* (New York: Crown Forum, 2004) 21.

45   Parents Television Council, Christopher Gildemeister, "Faith in a Box: Entertainment Television & Religion 2005-2006," http://www.parentstv.org/PTC/publications/ reports/religionstudy06/exsummary.asp (Viewed 12/18/07)

46   Colleen Raezler, "A Modern-Day Stoning?!? *Cold Case* Smears Christian Kids," Culture and Media Institute, October 1, 2007, http://www.cultureandmediainstitute.org/articles/2007/20071001183651.aspx (Viewed 12/18/07)

47   The Barna Group, "Surprisingly Few Adults Outside of Christianity Have Positive Views of Christians," December 3, 2002, http://www.barna.org/FlexPage.aspx?Page= BarnaUpdate&BarnaUpdateID=127 (Viewed 12/18/07)

48   Ibid.

49   Epic Stories of the Bible, "The Ten Commandments Challenge: 10 Commandments Study" (9/2007 Kelton Research and 10 Commandments Commission), http://www.epicstoriesofthebible.com/challenge.php (Viewed 12/18/07)

50   Classic Movies, "The Motion Picture Production Code of 1930 (Hays Code)," http://www.classicmovies.org/articles/blhayscode.htm (Viewed 12/18/07)

51   Quoted in Michael Medved, *Hollywood vs. America* (New York: Harper Perennial, 1992) 282.

52   Joseph Farah, *Taking America Back* (Nashville, Tenn.: WND Books, 2003) 8-9.

53   David M. Halbfinger, "Jack Valenti, Confidant of Presidents and Stars, Dies at 85," *The New York Times*, April 26, 2007, http://www.nytimes.com/2007/04/26/ obituaries/27valenticndcnd.html?ex=1335240000&en=0c82f3f4ae6348d6&ei= 5090&partner=rssuserland&emc=rss (Viewed 12/18/07)

54   Tom Flannery, "Hollywood—Back to the Future," reprinted in Ted Baehr and Pat Boone, *The Culture-Wise Family* (Ventura, Calif.: Regal Books, 2007) 130-131.

55   Michael Medved, *Hollywood vs. America* (New York: Harper Perennial, 1992) 283.

56   Ted Baehr and Pat Boone, *The Culture-Wise Family* (Ventura, Calif.: Regal Books, 2007) 133.

57   Jody Eldred, "Living and Working in a Spiritual Ghetto," *Whistleblower* 15, No. 11 (November 2006) 10.

58   Quoted in William J. Federer, *America's God and Country* (Coppell, Tex.: FAME Publishing, Inc., 1994) 460.

59   D. James Kennedy and Jerry Newcombe, *Lord of All* (Wheaton, Ill.: Crossway Books, 2005) 294.

60   Jeremy Leaming, "The Company They Keep: Coral Ridge Reaches Out To Christian Reconstructionist Fringe," Americans United for Separation of Church and State, November 19, 2007, http://blog.au.org/2007/11/19/the-company-they-keep-coral-ridge-reaches-out-to-christian-reconstructionist-fringe/ (Viewed 12/18/07)

61   *The One with Aldacron*, "Coral Ridge Ministries CEO Suggests Members Drown Atheists," October 18, 2007 http://aldacron.net/blog/2007/10/18/coral-ridge-ministries-ceo-suggests-members-drown-atheists/ (Viewed 12/18/07)

62   Nancy Pearcey, *Total Truth* (Wheaton, Ill.: Crossway Books, 2004) 22.

63   Mark Morford, "The Sum of All Fears: Organized Religion," *San Francisco Chronicle*, November 30, 2007, http://www.sfgate.com/cgibin/article.cgi?f=/c/a/2007/11/30/DDLRTKN1M.DTL&hw=Mark+Morford&sn=001&sc=1000 (Viewed 12/18/07)

64   Noel Sheppard, "Media Analyst Defends Rosie O'Donnell's 'Radical Christianity' Comments," NewsBusters, September 15, 2006, http://newsbusters.org/node/7656 (Viewed 12/18/07)

65   Justice Hugo Black wrote in a footnote to his opinion in *Torcaso v. Watkins*, 367 U.S. 488 (1961), the following: "Among religions in this country which do not teach what would generally be considered a belief in the existence of God are Buddhism, Taoism, Ethical Culture, Secular Humanism, and others." http://caselaw.lp.findlaw.com/cgi-bin/getcase.pl?court=us&vol=367&invol=488 (Viewed 12/21/2007)

66   The pilot episode *alone* cost $5 million to produce. Source: *Business Week*, "The Show Within A Show At NBC," July 31, 2006, http://www.businessweek.com/magazine/content/06_31/b3995085.htm (Viewed 12/18/07)

67   *The Hollywood Reporter*, "Season Ratings," Week 11, Dec. 3-9, Source: Nielsen Media Research, http://www.hollywoodreporter.com/hr/television/ratings/index.jsp (Viewed 12/18/07)

68   Baehr and Boone, *Culture-Wise Family*, 135.

69   Daniel Radosh, "The Good Book Business: Why publishers love the Bible," *The New Yorker*, December 18, 2006, http://www.newyorker.com/archive/2006/12/18/061218fa_fact1

70   Leftbehind.com, http://www.leftbehind.com/ (Viewed 12/18/07)

71   WaterBrook Multnomah Publishing Group, *The Prayer of Jabez, 5th Anniversary Edition*, "Story Behind the Book," http://www.randomhouse.com/waterbrook/catalog/display.pperl?isbn=9781590524756 (Viewed 12/18/07)

72   The Book Blog at ReadersRead.com, "The Purpose Driven Book Sales," http://www.readersread.com/cgi-bin/bookblog.pl?bblog=410051 (Viewed 12/18/07)

73   John Pollock, *Wilberforce* (Batavia, Ill.: Lion Publishing, 1977) 307.

74   D. James Kennedy, "Will the Church Forget," Coral Ridge Ministries.

75   Tad Friend, "Abstract: Mickey Mouse Club," *The New Yorker*, April 24, 2000, p. 212, http://www.newyorker.com/archive/2000/04/24/2000_04_24_212_TNY_LIBRY_000020731 (Viewed 12/18/07)

76   Conde Nast *Portfolio.com*, "The Walt Disney Company," http://www.portfolio.com/resources/company-profiles/91 (Viewed 12/18/07)

77   Sterling Rome, "Anchors Away," Catholic Education Resource Center, April 2, 2001, http://www.catholiceducation.org/articles/media/me0022.html (Viewed 12/18/07)

78   Frank Newport and Joseph Carroll, "Another Look at Evangelicals in America Today," The Gallup Organization, December 2, 2005, http://www.gallup.com/poll/20242/Another-Look-Evangelicals-America-Today.aspx (Viewed 12/18/07)

79   See, for example, Charles Colson and Nancy Pearcey, *How Now Shall We Live?* (Wheaton, Ill.: Tyndale House, 1999); David A. Noebel, *Understanding the Times* (Eugene, Oreg.: Harvest House, 1991); D. James Kennedy and Jerry Newcombe, *Lord of All* (Wheaton, Ill.: Crossway Books, 2005); Nancy Pearcey, *Total Truth* (Wheaton, Ill.: Crossway Books, 2004).

80   Charles Colson and Nancy Pearcey, *How Now Shall We Live?* (Wheaton, Ill.: Tyndale House, 1999) 14.

81   Colson and Pearcey, *How Now Shall We Live?* 14.

82   These were presented in a series essays titled, *A Christian View of God and the World*.

You can view this material on the Internet at the Calvin College Christian Classics Ethereal Library, http://www.ccel.org/ccel/orr/view.viii.html

83   Kennedy and Newcombe, *Lord of All*, 19. Dr. Kennedy and Jerry Newcombe credited the theologian Hermann Dooyeweerd with originating the concept of "sphere sovereignty."

84   Kennedy and Newcombe, *Lord of All*, 22.

85   Colson and Pearcey, *How Now Shall We Live?* 22.

86   Quoted from TeachingAmericanHistory.org, Abraham Lincoln, "The Perpetuation of Our Political Institutions," January 27, 1838, Address to the Young Men's Lyceum of Springfield, Ill., http://www.teachingamericanhistory.org/library/index.asp?document=157 (Viewed 12/18/07)

87   Albert L. Winseman, "Americans Have Little Doubt God Exists," The Gallup Organization, December 13, 2005, http://www.gallup.com/poll/20437/Americans-Little-Doubt-God-Exists.aspx (Viewed 12/18/07)

88   The Barna Group, "Most Americans Take Well-Known Bible Stories at Face Value," October 21, 2007, http://www.barna.org/FlexPage.aspx?Page=BarnaUpdate&Barna UpdateID=282 (Viewed 12/18/07)

89   Hugh Hewitt, *Blog* (Nashville, Tenn.: Thomas Nelson, Inc., 2005) 37-41. (MSM is Mr. Hewitt's designation for the "mainstream media." The superscript "th" in Rathergate is a tongue-in-cheek reference to the fact that the forged memos had superscripted those two letters, yet most typewriters of that era did not have that functionality.

90   CBS News, "Dan Rather Statement on Memos," September 20, 2004, http://www.cbsnews.com/stories/2004/09/20/politics/main644546.shtml (Viewed 12/18/07)

91   Howard Kurtz, "After Blogs Got Hits, CBS Got a Black Eye," *The Washington Post*, September 20, 2004, p. C01, http://www.washingtonpost.com/wp-dyn/articles/A34153-2004Sep19.html (Viewed 12/18/07)

92   Helen Leggatt, "Godtube.com U.S.'s fastest growing website," BizReport, September 18, 2007, http://www.bizreport.com/2007/09/Godtubecom_uss_fastest_growing_website.html (Viewed 12/18/07)

93   Houghton Mifflin Trade and Reference Division, Press Release, *The God Delusion*, http://www.houghtonmifflinbooks.com/booksellers/press_release/delusion/ (Viewed 12/18/07)

94   D. James Kennedy, *Why I Believe* (Nashville, Tenn.: Thomas Nelson, Inc., 2005) 141-155.

95   Suzy Bausch, "Nielsen//NetRatings Announces March U.S. Search Share Rankings," Nielsen//NetRatings, April 23, 2007, http://www.nielsen-netratings.com/pr/pr_070423.pdf (Viewed 12/18/07)

96   Frank Ahrens, "$2 Million Airtime, $13 Ad," *The Washington Post*, January 31, 2007, http://www.washingtonpost.com/wp-dyn/content/article/2007/01/30/AR200701 3001534.html (Viewed 12/18/07)

97   Laurie Petersen, "Internet Ad Spending Set To Overtake All Other Media By 2011: VSS," MediaPostPublications, August 7, 2007, http://publications.mediapost.com/index.cfm?fuseaction=Articles.san&s=65282&Nid=3301...%208/7/2007 (Viewed 12/18/07)

98   Source: ReachLocal, Inc.

99   Source: ReachLocal, Inc.

100   Jerry Ropelato, "Internet Pornography Statistics," Internet Filter Review, http://internet-filter-review.toptenreviews.com/internet-pornography-statistics.html#anchor4 (Viewed 12/18/07)

101   Jason Collum, "Pornography: A Woman's Struggle Too," *American Family Association*

Journal, March, 2004, http://www.afajournal.org/2004/march/304pornography.asp (Viewed 12/18/07)

102   *Reason* magazine reported in May of 2006 that there were 185,000 outlets in the U.S. that sold lottery tickets, while there were only 13,700 franchises that sell the Big Mac. Greg Beato, "Sin Cities on a Hill," *Reasononline*, May, 2006, http://www.reason.com/news/show/36647.html (Viewed 12/18/07)

103   American Gaming Association, "Industry Information, State Information: Statistics," http://www.americangaming.org/Industry/state/statistics.cfm (Viewed 12/18/07)

104   National Council on Problem Gambling, "Problem Gamblers: How widespread is problem gambling in the U.S.?" http://www.ncpgambling.org/i4a/pages/Index.cfm?pageID=3315#widespread (Viewed 12/17/07)

105   American Gaming Association, "Industry Information, State Information: Statistics," http://www.americangaming.org/Industry/factsheets/issues_detail.cfv?id=17 (Viewed 12/17/07)

106   Robert Schwaneberg and Josh Margolin, "Opponents of gay marriage launch all-out N.J. campaign," *The Star-Ledger*, November 29, 2007, http://www.nj.com/news/ledger/jersey/index.ssf?/base/news-8/1196319518194970.xml&coll=1 (Viewed 12/17/07)

SUGGESTED READING

Ted Baehr and Pat Boone, *The Culture-Wise Family* (Ventura, CA: Regal Books, 2007)

William J. Bennett, *The Index of Leading Cultural Indicators* (New York, NY: Broadway Books, 1999)

L. Brent Bozell III, *Weapons of Mass Distortion* (New York, NY: Crown Forum, 2004)

Charles Colson and Nancy Pearcey, *How Now Shall We Live?* (Wheaton, IL: Tyndale House, 1999)

Joseph Farah, *Stop the Presses!* (Los Angeles, CA: World Ahead Media, 2007)

Hugh Hewitt, *Blog* (Nashville, TN: Thomas Nelson, Inc., 2005)

D. James Kennedy and Jerry Newcombe, *Lord of All* (Wheaton, IL: Crossway Books, 2005)

D. James Kennedy, *Why I Believe* (Nashville, TN: Thomas Nelson, Inc., 2005)

David Kupelian, *The Marketing of Evil* (Nashville, TN: WND Books, 2005)

Michael Medved, *Hollywood Vs. America* (New York, NY: Harper Perennial, 1992)

David A. Noebel, *Understanding The Times* (Eugene, OR: Harvest House, 1991)

Nancy Pearcey, *Total Truth* (Wheaton, IL: Crossway Books, 2004)

INDEX

202

NOTES

NOTES

NOTES

NOTES